Faithful to the Vision

Mother Cecile (Annie Cecile Ramsbottom Isherwood)
founder of the Community of the Resurrection of our Lord, and first Mother.
The inspiration behind the Training College.

Faithful to the Vision

A History of the
Grahamstown Teachers' Training College
1894 –1975

Eric Kelly

First edition, first impression 2018
Second impression 2025

Published in South Africa on behalf of the author by
NISC (Pty) Ltd, PO Box 377, Grahamstown, 6140, South Africa

ISBN 978-1-920033-27-9 (softcover)
ISBN 978-1-991458-13-1 (PDF)
ISBN 978-1-991458-14-8 (ePub)

Design, typesetting and layout: NISC (Pty) Ltd
Cover design: Advanced Design Group
Photographs: ©Tony Dold, unless otherwise indicated

Cover photograph: Canterbury House, built in 1907 as a hostel for students of the Grahamstown Teachers' Training College and named in recognition of the financial support received by the College from the Archbishop of Canterbury

Dedication

And there went forth bands of teachers *"whose hearts God had touched"*.

1 Sam 10:26

This book is dedicated to all the teachers who went out from the College in the years of its existence, as a thanksgiving for their contribution to education in Southern Africa.

Contents

Preface ix

CHAPTER 1   In the beginning...1

CHAPTER 2   The Grahamstown Teacher Training School
1894–1904 9

CHAPTER 3   TC under Sister Clare 1904–1920.......................21

CHAPTER 4   TC under Sister Kate 1911–1931........................44

CHAPTER 5   TC under Sister Frances Mary 1931–1946 50

CHAPTER 6   TC under Sister Truda 1947–1957 and
1961–1962 75

CHAPTER 7   TC under Sister Virginia 1962–1969.................105

CHAPTER 8   TC under Mrs Enid Craig and
Miss Bridget Pilson 1970–1975 115

CHAPTER 9   The lead-up to the closure of the College.........119

CHAPTER 10   The Diaspora 132

CHAPTER 11   Conclusion...147

Appendix 152

Preface

The present work is based on a thesis written for the degree of Doctor of Philosophy of Rhodes University[1]. The thesis is available for reference on the Rhodes University Library website. For this reason, and to avoid the plethora of footnotes occurring in the thesis, no references have been provided in the book. When the Grahamstown Training College (TC) closed in 1975, all the archives were moved to the Cory Library for Historical Research at Rhodes University. These archives were then catalogued by a Librarian, Mr Michael Berning, and so are easily available on application. It was clear to the present writer that this material had not ever been researched.

When I was a student at Rhodes University from 1957 to 1960, TC was, to the outsider at any rate, a flourishing institution. It was clearly a College with more than a country-wide reputation. When I returned to Grahamstown some fifty-five years later after my retirement as an Anglican Priest, I decided that I would like to ensure that the memory of this notable institution was preserved as more than just catalogued archives. I set about preparing for the higher degree. This preparation covered just over three years of continuous research work followed by a year writing up the material, and during that time I became thoroughly immersed in the history of the Training College. I also came to feel that I really knew some of the Sisters, especially the Sisters Principal. It was a fascinating experience.

It is my hope that those who read this book, especially Old Girls of the College, will enjoy what they read and find the journey as intriguing as I did. The closure of TC was a much lamented event. Whether this should have happened or not, I will leave the reader to decide. What becomes clear is that matters were not all they appeared to be on the surface. Be that as it may, Rhodes University, after purchasing the TC campus, spent a great deal of money refurbishing and renovating the buildings, and even today the special atmosphere of generations of prayer may be felt on St Peter's campus.

---

1   *A History of the Grahamstown Teachers' Training College 1894–1975.* Thesis submitted to Rhodes University for the degree of Doctor of Philosphy, by Leonard Eric Kelly, November 2016

Acknowledgments

Mike Schramm and his team at NISC for preparing the manuscript for publication

Tony Dold, Curator of the Schonland Herbarium, for the photographs of the College buildings

The Mother Superior and the Sisters of the Community of the Resurrection of Our Lord for all their assistance, and for the copy of the photograph of Mother Cecile which hangs at St Peter's Home in Donkin Street

The Old Girls and others who assisted me when I was preparing my thesis on which this book is based

Malcolm Hacksley and Wendy Jacobson for reading the manuscript and for their valuable and helpful advice and suggestions

Our son Paul Adrian Kelly for his assistance in making the publication and printing of this book possible, and our daughter Janet Erica Viljoen who has been a source of encouragement from the outset of this research

My wife Jean without whose help and encouragement and persistence this book would never have seen the light of day. Jean was indeed the editor-in-chief!

Canterbury House (corner of Grey/Beaufort and Somerset Streets). Now a women's residence in Allan Webb Hall, Rhodes University

The teaching block (1904) from Grey Street. Now part of the Faculty of Education, Rhodes University

Exterior of the Memorial Hall (1909) from the gardens

The Library block (1940) from Grey Street. It is now part of the Faculty of Education, Rhodes University

Interior of the Mother Cecile Memorial Hall (1909). Now the dining hall for the students of Allan Webb Hall of Rhodes University. The portraits on the back wall are of Mother Cecile and Bishop Webb

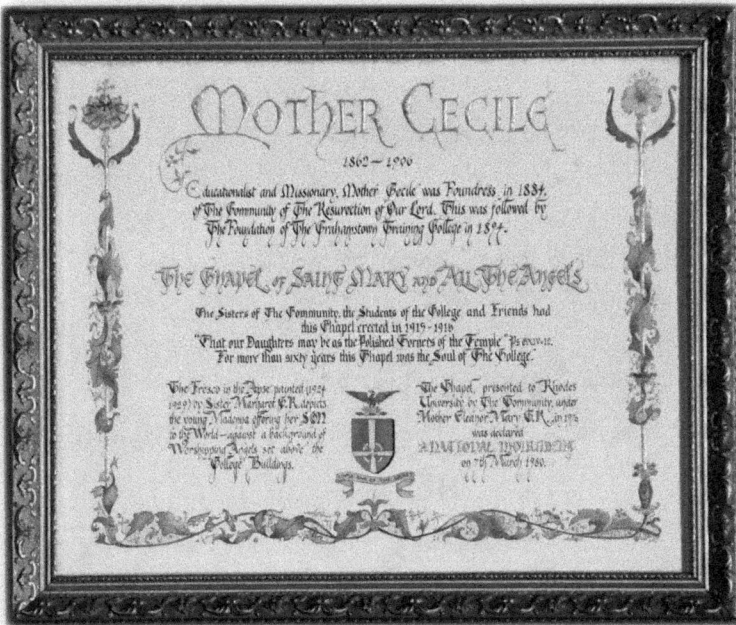

The Illuminated Scroll recording the gift of the Chapel by the Sisters of the Community of the Resurrection of our Lord

The Chapel of St Mary and All the Angels. Grahamstown Training College (1916)

Interior of the Chapel of St Mary and All the Angels. Now the University Chapel

CHAPTER 1

In the beginning...

CECILE ISHERWOOD ARRIVED in Grahamstown in November 1883. She came in response to an appeal by the newly-appointed Bishop of Grahamstown, Allan Beecher Webb, whom she had heard preach in St Peter's, Eaton Square, London in July 1883. He asked women who were free to do so to come out to the Cape Colony to do church work.

Bishop Webb knew the place and value of women's work in the growing but scattered white population of the Colony and more particularly of his diocese. The most important aspect of this work was education. He argued that the missionary value of this work could not be overestimated. In his opinion the education of girls in country places was more necessary than it was even in England. The women he recruited should not only be able to lead society but to give a tone to the society in which they worked. He was convinced that the answer lay in the setting up of a Community of Sisters.

The Bishop was careful to explain that he wished to recruit women with strength of character and of personality. If one considers the women who responded to the call in those early days one feels that he got what he wanted in good measure. Many of these women later joined the community of sisters set up in Grahamstown.

When Cecile Isherwood responded to the Bishop's appeal she saw it as a call from God. Before leaving England for the Cape she asked to be made a deaconess of the Church of England. Her wish was that her whole life might be pledged to the Lord's service. With like-minded companions she sailed from England on 4 October 1883.

When this group of women arrived in Grahamstown willing and eager to carry out what was expected of them, they were at first employed in district work. This included training white and African girls as home-makersl, visiting the sick, caring for women and children, and evangelising, a task that included a measure of teaching. There was an urgency about this work and it brought Miss Isherwood into contact with young orphaned waifs and strays some of whom were forced to spend their nights in the town gaol in the company of hardened criminals.

Along with this work Cecile Isherwood had not lost sight of her initial intention of serving the Lord and so, under Bishop Webb's guidance, she prepared to dedicate her life as a Sister of Mercy. She was admitted as a Novice on 25 March 1884. Here was a young woman in a strange country conscious of the joy and wonder of her call and utterly dependent on the strength of God. This was the beginning of the Community of the Resurrection of Our Lord (CR). At the age of twenty-one she became Sister Cecile the first member and the first Mother of the Community. This deeply spiritual dimension was to undergird the whole life of the work of training teachers which she started and the other works which the CR undertook.

Some months after Mother Cecile's arrival in Grahamstown, she started a small school in a building in Anglo-African Street, but in 1884 the school was transferred to a cottage in the grounds of Eden Grove, a property which she had purchased as a base for the community. The school became St Peter's School. By 1887 attendance at the school averaged 50 children. To staff this school and others she started at this time, Mother Cecile made use of the pupil-teacher system. Mother Florence, the second Superior of the Community, recalled the rejoicings there were in 1887 because the three pupil-teachers admitted from St Peter's school for the Elementary Examination had all passed, with one of them coming sixth in the Colony.

In 1888 two of these candidates, Bertha Mingay and Emily Jordan, passed the T3 examination (which was the qualifying examination) high in the first grade, third and eleventh in the Colony respectively with honours in English and Dutch. These results were a splendid start in the training of teachers and it is mentioned that the good results were kept up in the succeeding years. Later Bertha Mingay started a small school in the building which is the DRC hall today. Through her steady, thorough work it flourished so rapidly that it eventually became the present popular Victoria Girls' Primary School in Beaufort Street.

There were five pupil-teachers in 1891. They were prepared by Sister Margaret. Sister Clare later acknowledged that Sister Margaret had taught her to give attention to practical detail, a training she had never previously received.

In 1893 Mother Cecile wrote to the Superintendent General of Education (SGE), Dr Thomas Muir, requesting that St Peter's school be placed under government inspection, as what was then known as a third-class Church School. At that time the staff consisted of Miss Goodlatte (later Sister Clare) who joined the staff in 1891, Miss Erskine Cole (later Sister Christine), Sister Aline and Miss Custance.

In 1894 the training of pupil-teachers was given serious attention; the classes were at first attached to St Peter's School and the Good Shepherd Mission School where practice in teaching was possible. It was in that year that the upper class began a separate existence as a training school out of which was to emerge the Training College. This was an immediate success and quite clearly met an urgent need.

The Community Sisters set a high standard, a fact acknowledged by others. Mother Cecile had the uncanny ability to inspire people to be and to do their best. Part of the influence that she exercised stemmed from her determination to be *au fait* with whatever it was she initiated. She set herself to master the principles and general routine of all the work undertaken. She spared herself no toil, shrank from no drudgery, that might be necessary to enable her to understand the difficulties and appreciate the labours of her subordinates. Thus in 1894 when the first vacation course aimed at neglected country teachers was held in Grahamstown, Mother Cecile enrolled as a student and complied in every minute requirement asked of the participants.

Dr Thomas Muir served from 1892 to 1915 as Superintendent General of Education (SGE) – a non-ministerial post in the Colonial Administration. He was very aware of the need for professional training of teachers. On his first tour of the Colony outside Cape Town, he held meetings at many places in the hope that private bodies would aid the government in filling the need for training institutions for teachers. He addressed such a meeting in Grahamstown which was a growing education centre in the eastern part of the Colony.

What exactly did Dr Muir envisage for Grahamstown? In his mind were these schemes: that there should be a high school for girls; a high school for boys; a kindergarten and a large elementary school for the poorer classes of the population. He felt that there should be a teacher training school, not only for Grahamstown but for the eastern districts of the Colony as a whole; in his mind was the provision of a university college in Grahamstown.

The seed is sown

Mother Cecile was present at that meeting addressed by Dr Muir in the City Hall in Grahamstown on 11 July 1894. Dr Muir spoke of the urgent need for a teacher training school in the eastern Cape. Mother Cecile immediately saw the power for good such a training school could be for the future teachers in South Africa. She was the only person present at the meeting who responded to the call for ideas. By then the Sisters were already training pupil-teachers for their own schools so the nucleus of a teacher-training school was in existence.

At St Peter's School the pupil-teachers and other students had been working for their Teaching Certificates under Sister Margaret who was the third woman to join the community. The Community would have preferred to continue with the care and instruction of the poor and needy in the town and beyond, but Mother Cecile's enthusiasm soon captured the hearts of the teachers among the Sisters.

It was not to be a smooth ride. Was Mother Cecile's enthusiasm running away with her? Many prominent educationalists opposed the idea. Canon John Espin the Headmaster of St Andrew's College told Mother Cecile that her project was impossible. Canon Espin's son, speaker at Founder's Day in 1947, was to recall: "Mother Cecile loved to accomplish the impossible. I wonder if Mother Cecile ever dreamt when she planted her tiny seed that it would develop into the mighty institution the Training College has become and its influence through the teachers it has trained would spread through South Africa? I believe she did, for if ever a woman had vision Mother Cecile had."

Sir William Solomon, judge president and a friend to Mother Cecile, never forgot his first interview with her when she went to see him soon after his arrival in Grahamstown. She hoped to enlist his sympathy and co-operation in the work of the training school. He had feared that the Mother might not be sufficiently broad-minded to satisfy his somewhat liberal views of religion and education. He came to admire greatly the bravery and courage which she displayed in those early days. With hindsight he acknowledged that there was never a more broad-minded Christian woman than Mother Cecile. He came to see it as a privilege to have been associated with her in her work and to have been able to give her some support and encouragement in whatever she undertook.

Clearly what Mother Cecile was proposing was to many of her supporters an impossible undertaking. She envisaged a training school provided by, belonging to, and controlled by, a Community of Anglican Sisters. It was to be a place where girls of English and Dutch backgrounds were to be trained as teachers; these girls could be of any religious denomination, as all were to be welcome; and as trained teachers they would be sent out to the country schools of the land.

Miss EB Hawkins speaking at a Founder's Day Assembly, recalled that in those early days when even food and clothing were hard to come by, Mother Cecile planned and worked as though she had unlimited financial resources at her command. She let nothing check her or bar the way to the realisation of the vision she had seen – a vision not of fame and honour for herself but for the glory of God and the lasting good of the people of this country.

Dr LS Jameson, Prime Minister of the Cape, addressing the students at Prize-Giving in December 1904, explained that Mother Cecile had insisted that he should come and commented that they no doubt knew even better than he that what Mother Cecile insisted upon generally came about. Sir William Solomon believed that no-one was able to resist that remarkable personality when she chose to exert her persuasive powers.

The Mother won over her opposition and within a few days wrote to Dr Muir offering to supply just such a training school as he wanted, if he would promise her government grants.

Mother Cecile was undoubtedly a leader with tremendous ability. As such she was also subject to the criticisms levelled at leaders. In her own mind she was clear about the aims to be achieved and, if in pursuit of those aims, she appeared at times intolerant of methods or individuals moving more slowly than herself, those around her came to understand that this was only the shadow cast by that God-given power which made her the unique force she became both in Church and Nation. Mother Cecile responded to Dr Muir's appeal without any thought of the toil and trouble entailed and saw only what could be accomplished.

When Dr Muir visited Mother Cecile he realised that he had met a personality with whom to reckon and was not slow to come to terms with her, promising then and there the genuine support he never afterwards failed to give. He was attracted by her zeal and ability. In 1909, on a later visit to the College and when addressing the students, Dr Muir referred to Mother Cecile as a woman who had a love for everything good and true and beautiful. He described her as a woman with an utter devotion to duty, one who was never satisfied until she had done her best and had given all she could. The editor of the College Magazine wrote that Dr Muir became a firm friend of Mother Cecile's schools because he had found in her a true fellow-labourer, an enthusiastic educator and a most zealous and untiring colleague in the great task to which he was devoted. And in turn the College received from Dr Muir and his officers in the Education Department generous recognition, kindly patience, fair and just dealing, valuable guidance and help in the work.

Dr Muir had to arrive at a compromise with Mother Cecile. He had to administer an Act of Parliament which did not take churches into consideration. It was not because he had no wish for religious instruction to be given but his ideal was to have Training Schools free from any Church management. The Education Act No 13 of 1865 was to govern education in the Cape Colony for forty years. The conditions of Aid to Schools laid down that religious instruction was to be given for one hour per day, but parents would have the option of withdrawing their children during that hour. Further, the government was authorised to inspect all schools which received any aid from the treasury. This inspection was to include buildings, classrooms, and a thorough examination of all the children in the various classes before promotion, and it was to happen at least once a year. The Act also placed the Pupil-Teacher system on a firmer financial basis.

Between 1892 and 1920, thirteen colleges/schools for the training of teachers were opened in the Cape Province. (Cape Town Training College, 1893; Wellington Training College, 1893; Grahamstown Training College, 1894; Stellenbosch Training School, 1908; Robertson Training School, 1912; Paarl Training College, 1913; Kimberley Training School, 1913; Cradock Training School, 1913; King William's Town Training School, 1914; Steynsburg Training School, 1914; Oudtshoorn Training School, 1914; Graaff-Reinet Training School, 1916; Uitenhage Training School, 1919.) All except one of these colleges originated in the offices of the Department of Education in Cape Town.

Only one of those training colleges can claim to have been the brain-child of a young woman. It was an amazing achievement and the School, later College, was to have a lifespan of 81 years before closure in 1975. Sister Kate described the Grahamstown Teacher Training College (TC) as a unique educational development. It was to be a Government aided and inspected institution but privately owned. It was thus one of the first among many Aided European Training Institutions. This was Dr Muir's policy and it was the pattern on which Coloured and African as well as European, institutions were built up. Namely that the buildings were supplied by the Mission Institutions and the Government provided grants towards salaries, equipment and maintenance. (The Grahamstown Teacher Training College was traditionally referred to by its students and OGs as "TC" and this is how it will be referred to hereafter in the text.)

The Department of Education thus agreed at first to pay a proportion of the staff salaries, later to pay the whole of the salaries, but the property was privately owned by the Community and a Board of Trustees. The Community wished to receive no help from the Department in this respect in order that they might retain full control over the buildings. This could only be done if the property was privately owned and not built partly with Government Funds.

In 1894 the officially organised and sanctioned training of teachers in Grahamstown began. It has been said of Mother Cecile that she did great things for education but that her influence was even greater than her work. In April 1897 Dr Muir visited the College and expressed his full satisfaction with what he saw. The training school was more than coming up to expectation. At that time the principal was Sister Mary Ruth, and Miss Williamson, Miss Dyer and Miss Coates comprised the staff.

A serious challenge

Official recognition had been achieved but the training school was not out of the woods. It was run by the Sisters as a private enterprise and an Anglican institution although other denominations were welcome. It was subject to Departmental Inspection and the students wrote the official departmental examinations. Dr Muir was unhappy with this arrangement.

Dr Muir was in Grahamstown again for the official opening of the Boys' Public School in April 1899. In his speech on that occasion he said that his only regret regarding the training school at St Peter's was that it was not associated with Grahamstown as a whole. What he had in mind was a Grahamstown teacher training school. He appealed to the Grahamstown people to sink their differences and unite in creating such a school. At the same time Dr Muir was generous in his praise of what the Sisters were doing at St Peter's.

Canon John Espin then Chairman of the Advisory Board wrote to Mother Cecile, who was in Scotland at the time, that he had had a meeting with Dr Muir in Cape Town at the end of March 1899. They had discussed Dr Muir's plans for a training school/college in Grahamstown. Canon Espin had pointed out that a scheme carried out on such lines might involve the retirement of the Sisters, but Dr Muir did not want this to happen. Canon Espin advised that if this was what the people of Grahamstown really wanted the Sisters would have to accept it.

To allay fears that the training school was a narrow Anglican institution the Chairman of the Board had invited the Presbyterian Minister, the Rev. Mr W Liddle, and the Baptist Minister, the Rev. Mr GW Cross to join the Advisory Board. Mr Cross had no intention of accepting the invitation and pressed for consultation regarding a non-denominational training school.

In June 1899 a Public Meeting was called in the Council Chamber at the City Hall to discuss the proposals for the establishment of a training school for pupil-teachers in Grahamstown. It was chaired by the Mayor, Mr Henry Wood. The meeting was well attended. It was a representative and influential gathering, including many ladies.

After much discussion Dr Schonland suggested that a small Committee should be appointed to take the matter forward; this was agreed to. The Committee was to report back to a public meeting a fortnight later. The City Council endorsed the idea and agreed that an eligible piece of ground situated between Oatlands Road and Henry Street known as St George's Park should be granted for the desirable and important purpose. Nothing further was heard about such a scheme and the training school as already established remained in place.

It had been a close-run challenge but the policy at the training school continued to be to work with Dr Muir. Mother Cecile took note of what this could have meant to the training school. She immediately implemented an arrangement enabling Ministers of the different denominations to have "right of entry" to the training school so that they would be free to instruct students of their own denomination.

CHAPTER 2

The Grahamstown
Teacher Training School
1894–1904

IN JULY 1894 the Grahamstown Training School had opened with eight students: Annie Cogan, Noel E Gatonby, Beatrice Haigh, Lucy Jeffreys, Alice Smith, Amy Smith, Katie Winny, Gwynneth Wood. The Staff at the time included Sister Clare, Sister Marion, Sister Edith Mary, Miss Cromartie (the Principal of Diocesan School for Girls), Miss Erskine (who became Sister Mary Christian) and Miss Wallich.

The early years of the Community were years of sacrifice and struggle and of amazing fertility. Ventures were eagerly undertaken, helpers were attracted to the work and there was expansion in every direction. The Sisters began modestly, lived frugally and laboured unremittingly and disinterestedly for the good of others. Confidence in them and their work grew, more helpers arrived, and the generosity of their friends increased. It was observed that when Mother Cecile wanted money, money came. Not all who were admitted to the training school stayed the course. Remarks in the early registers record reasons for the withdrawal of students: dead; too young; unfit for teaching; wanted at home; gone to Rhodesia; loss of sight; unfit for study; left Africa.

The Grahamstown Training School was founded on definite principles: every student was accepted as an individual and not as a mere examination machine expected to produce the best results. At all times, it was the students' best interests that were paramount. Although the training school was to be an Anglican foundation, students of other religious bodies were welcome. It was intended that the training school should be seen and experienced as a true Christian home where the students would have the benefits of experiencing an example of a simple, healthy, Christian life.

From the beginning there was a good working relationship with the Education Department in Cape Town and these good relations were to exist until the final closure of the College in 1975.

Religious and cultural tolerance

From the outset Mother Cecile was adamant that girls other than Anglicans should be welcome as students and so take advantage of the professional teacher training offered. This was to remain the policy throughout the life of the institution. Girls of the Jewish faith were accepted and, even in the days before the ecumenical movement gathered momentum, Roman Catholics were also welcome including several groups of Roman Catholic Nuns for training. By 1918 the following denominations had been recorded in the Registers: English Church, Wesleyan, Presbyterian, Dutch Reformed Church, Congregationalist, Roman Catholic, Baptist, Lutheran, "Brethren", Salvation Army and "Church of Christ", and there were Jewish girls. Later special regulations were drawn up to allow Jewish students to attend Synagogue and Hillel House where those of the Jewish faith fraternised. In 1948 Felix Johnson became the first Roman Catholic student to be elected Senior Student. There is no record of an application ever having been received from a Muslim girl.

This tolerance extended to girls from Dutch backgrounds as well as English. Co-education of this character (i.e. Dutch and English) became general in South Africa later, but in the early years of the Training School it was an experiment which implied courage; and it was judged to be an unqualified success. Mother Cecile believed that nothing would so unite the two European races of this troubled land as co-operation between them on this matter of vital importance to the national life – namely education.

Mother Cecile therefore prepared all her rapidly-developing plans with the definite view of including the Dutch in whatever advantage her training school had to offer. To do this meant breaking away from the old tradition of Church Schools. She had to face great opposition over this and hold her own against criticism from those whose judgement she valued, as already mentioned. But her courage never failed, and she held her ground.

The early days of the Training School

In the Annual Newsletter of the Old Girls' Guild (OGG) in 1951 the Old Girls (OGs) recalled that the beginnings of TC were thoroughly Victorian. There were the restrictions of that age but there were also the benefits for there was more family life and many homely pleasures. Within the training school family, amusements and happiness had to be "home made" for transport was difficult, money was not plentiful, and outside entertainments were rare.

The students lived as one big family on intimate terms with the Mother Superior and the Sisters who cared for them and whose friendship the students valued. It must be remembered that the pupils of the early days were generally young girls for whom the conditions of school life were in many ways a novelty and therefore acceptable.

Initially the students lived with the Sisters in the house at Eden Grove which later became St Peter's Home. "Eden Grove" was the property acquired for the newly formed Community by Bishop Webb. It was part of what is today the St Peter's Campus of Rhodes University. There were several dilapidated buildings on the site, the coach house and stables, several outside rooms and the Cottage which was "home". Part of the existing Sisters' Chapel was the first building put up after the purchase, in 1886.

Mr and Mrs Huntly lived next door to the Sisters at Government House. Their grandson FH Holland, then a boy of ten, remembered how Mother Cecile used to drop in frequently through the private entrance between the two properties to talk over problems with Mrs Huntly his grandmother. This cultured woman, he believed, knew nothing about housekeeping, cooking, washing babies or any of the other difficulties she had to face in plenty when the House for pupils and orphans was started.

Mother Cecile aroused much admiration for the bravery and courage which she displayed at the time. In the early days of the Training School, the prospects of final success were by no means assured. In those days teaching was not an attractive career, especially as an alternative to the free open-air life of South Africa. To encourage parents to allow their daughters to attend the Training School, Mother Cecile toured the area by donkey-cart for weeks to find girls for the first classes for teacher training at St Peter's School. In times of difficulty her solution was always the same: "We must use our knees". It was in 1904 that the Department upgraded the Training School to a Training College, a move determined by the annual enrolment.

In 1954 when TC celebrated its Jubilee, the College Magazine described how the early students fifty years previously came from distant farms travelling by ox-wagon. At home they had been accustomed to ride bareback over the veld. They must have found the adjustment to a life governed by the constant call of bells and obedience to rules a difficult one. The standard of entrance to the Training School was Standard IV so nobody felt over-burdened with learning.

Each girl brought with her a cup, saucer, plate, knife, fork, spoon and bed-linen. The china tended to get broken, and the cutlery lost, so that by the end of the term there were not sufficient utensils to go round. Sleeping accommodation was in large open dormitories furnished with beds and with a big narrow wash-stand at one end of the room on which enamel wash-basins were arranged. A curtain against a small portion of the wall provided a limited hanging space for dresses. There were no bed-side lockers, no chairs, and no privacy whatsoever.

How teachers were trained

Before Dr Muir became SGE, a teacher's training lasted only one year. As late as 1897 girls entered the first-year course straight from Standard IV. When the Grahamstown Training School was first recognised there was great difficulty in keeping up the numbers in the different years and in persuading girls to go in for the training. Dr Muir was responsible for ensuring that professionalism became apparent; it was he who placed the training of teachers at the Cape on a sound and proper footing.

Between 1894 and 1896 the work of training at St Peter's Home was confined to the handful of pupil-teachers attached to the day schools under the care of the community. It was a three-year course. Students were required to study all subjects up to Standard VI and at the same time they taught in the school as pupil-teachers. During the years 1894–1896, 40 pupil-teachers were presented for the yearly exams; all passed, 30 in the first grade. Many of those early students came from farm schools or one-teacher schools at the age of 14 or 15 years.

At St Peter's Home much use was made of volunteers from Britain; women who volunteered to serve for a period in Grahamstown to assist the Sisters. In 1906 one such lay worker wrote to the English Helpers' Union (EHU), a group of well-wishers in the UK, describing her experiences. She mentioned that her work was mainly with the students especially the juniors aged between 14 and 17 years, the pupil-teachers in their second year, other students in their first year and the boarders or those who had not yet passed their sixth standard and were still at school.

She described the students as for the most part strong girls, excitable, full of life, and in her opinion, unaccustomed to discipline of any nature. She added that notwithstanding their wildness there was a certain powerful attractiveness in them. She felt that girls so full of life and strength held out rich promise for the future. For the most part their characters were strong, and though self-willed at that stage, capable of being splendidly ennobled if handled rightly.

At the time of writing the lay worker mentioned that the girls were thinking only of the holidays which began in June. For many of the students the journey home was such a long one that they only managed to go home once a year, if that, so holidays became great events. That year, 1906, about 18 girls would remain in College, so arrangements were made to give them as pleasant a time as possible.

The Training School opened in 1897 with 33 students; by 1899 the number had risen to over 60. In 1897 following on the increase of numbers and the prospect of further growth, the institution received recognition from the Education Department as a Training Centre. The Inspectors' Report for that year mentioned that the character of the work done by the GTS was of a high order indeed. After that, numbers grew, and the good success attained in examinations placed the work on a firm basis.

In 1903 the training of kindergarten and second class teachers was undertaken. Second class Teachers could teach both in primary schools and the lower standards of secondary schools. Third class teachers were primary school teachers only. Third class schools were primary schools; second class schools were secondary schools; first class schools were of a superior nature altogether. These were in the larger centres where it was possible to provide a more comprehensive education.

The pupil-teacher system remained in place though certain improvements were made. The SGE working through the Circuit Inspectors ensured that care was taken that pupil-teachers received a suitable general education and proper professional instruction; that they had a certain amount of daily practice in teaching without being reduced to the status of drudges; and that their progress was tested yearly by an oral and written examination and by teaching in the presence of an inspector.

The minimum age for admission as a pupil-teacher was thirteen, and the pupil was required to sign up for a three-year apprenticeship. The entrance requirements changed over the years: in 1894, it was necessary to have passed Standard IV; in 1899 Standard V; in 1901 Standard VI; in 1909 Standard VII; and in 1920 Standard VIII. The low fixing of the admission standard at the outset was a matter of necessity, for better qualified candidates would not have been found. The raising of the standard for admission showed gradual improvement over the years. A formal agreement was signed between the pupil-teacher and the Chairman of the Board of Management.

An early student, indeed a foundation student, Miss Lucy Jeffreys, spoke at Founder's Day in 1933 and reminisced about her years as a pupil-teacher: "We had to teach in the morning, attend class in the afternoon, and do our preparation in the evening. On Saturday we had to attend classes for Needlework, Singing and Blackboard Work, and turn up again on Saturday afternoon if we were told to do so... Before we left in 1896, Mother Cecile addressed us with the following inspiring words: As teachers do your duty through prayer, and remember that LSD (=sterling) means Life, Service, Discipline, not pounds, shillings and pence... In my time Mother Cecile had sisters in the Community who were excellent, in fact, remarkable, teachers, and they helped her to carry on her noble work and shared equally in the building-up of this great College. We owe them an everlasting debt of gratitude for their faithful services given to South Africa."

The Inspection carried out on 8–9 May 1899 reported on a most capable staff and the zeal and industry displayed. The general tone and discipline was excellent. The Training School was already proving itself as an institution with which to reckon. A total of 119 students had already been presented for the Government Examination with only one failure and a large majority had passed in the first grade.

Two ex-students were employed in training pupil-teachers in Native Normal Schools to the evident satisfaction of the Education Department. The Normal School was the specialised school for the training of teachers. Initially the pupil-teacher system was in place; later the whole function of the Normal School was to produce professionally trained teachers. The Annual Report of the SGE for 1898 stated: "The Training School at Grahamstown has made excellent progress and, in the examinations, has done even better than in 1897. Of the 57 pupils presented, not one failed, and more than half were placed in the first grade. There is no school which promises to have a brighter future."

There were to be many problems during those early years, culminating in the South African War of 1899–1902 which affected the smooth running of the establishment and its survival. It was said however that the word "failure" did not feature in Mother Cecile's vocabulary. "It says something for the grit of our Colonial girls," she wrote, "that we presented 62 for the Government Examination in 1900 and 61 passed – 38 of that number being first grade – and this during the strain of the war. One student alone lost seven of her own near kith and kin." The effects of the war were nonetheless to be felt as the General Report on the Pupil-Teachers' Examinations in March 1903 revealed: "As regards the quality of the work, the Grahamstown Training School is not yet up to its usual very high standard..."

It was the earnest hope of the Community Sisters that the healing of the wounds of war and the building up of a loyal and industrious population in the country lay with the younger generation and those responsible for teaching them. Initially the first pupil-teachers were under the direction of Mother Cecile.

Mr Rankin as Principal

In 1900 Mr EH Rankin was appointed as Principal of the Training School, as it was the practice at the time to appoint men. This was in response to a directive from the SGE Dr Muir that a male teacher should be appointed, having special charge of one of the classes and exercising general supervision over the whole. In a handwritten and personally signed memorandum from the Bishop of Grahamstown, Charles Cornish, dated September 14, 1899 and intended as an advertisement for the position of Principal at the Training School, the Bishop described the Training School as one of the most important educational institutions in South Africa.

The Bishop considered that the position offered great opportunities of useful and interesting work with great future possibilities if properly developed. It was an opportunity for a man of grit and power, content to wait, lay solid foundations and build slowly. Speaking at the Founder's Day in 1933, Mr Rankin, the guest speaker, explained how his appointment had come about. He described Mother Cecile as a skilful craftsman who wanted to make a beautiful article, one of the conditions under which she laboured being that she must use a certain tool. That tool which she took and used for four and a half years was himself; but when it became clear that another instrument was better for the purpose, his association with this place came to an end. The innuendo here would suggest that Mr Rankin's departure from the Training School was on less than amicable terms.

On his arrival in Grahamstown in 1900 Mother Cecile, full of charm and enthusiasm, showed Mr Rankin round the training school. He was surprised to find that the entire school consisted of only three rooms with rather poor furniture, three blackboards and a few wall maps. "Mother Cecile said: 'Come and see me if you want anything.' So, at the end of the week I came again bringing a list of what I wanted. I can see her face now as she said: 'I know you want all these things, but you can't have them. I'll tell you two things that you must have: first, faith in the future and success of this institution, and second, patience.'"

The start of the Training College campus

In 1897 the Training School had opened with 33 students and the central block of St Peter's Home was given over entirely to them. Within two to three years the numbers reached just over 60 and a new building was urgently needed. The Inspectors had always accepted what was available. The report for 1897 considered the classrooms roomy and generally comfortable (perhaps a little draughty), the furniture and general equipment sufficient. In 1898, the classrooms were described as airy and comfortable.

Funds could not be collected until after the South African War, when Mother Cecile visited England in 1902. During her visit she encouraged the reorganisation of the English Helpers' Union specifically as a Fund-Raising Group of Friends who were interested in furthering the work of the Community in Grahamstown. They did this and more.

Mother Cecile was indifferent to comfort; if the wind and the rain were kept out that was all that mattered! She found it difficult to come to terms with the plans to build costly permanent buildings. Mother Cecile had a great fear of debt and the trust deeds of the Community were so drawn up that the power of mortgage was severely restricted. Once she realised the force of the argument in favour of a fine group of buildings worthy of a great Training College, she threw herself into fund raising with characteristic enthusiasm. Within a few months of her arrival in England so zealously did she plead the cause "from Land's End to John o' Groats" that a sum of £5000 was raised.

Mother Cecile returned to Africa in May 1903. She informed the Finance Committee on 23 July that the Community had bought the property in Grey Street known as The Grotto for the sum of £2300. Here it was proposed to erect new classrooms for the Training School to cost (approximately) £2500. It was here that on 31 August the Foundation Stone of the new College was laid by Bishop Wilkinson. In May 1904 the building was opened by the SGE Dr Muir. On the Foundation stone are the words:

> This building is a gift from the Mother Country to help forward our common hope, That our daughters may be as the polished corners of the temple.

The words reflect Mother Cecile's hope for the formation of noble characters and Christian tolerance among her students. Her spiritual ideal was no less seen in the motto which was evolved later, stressing this ministry "unto one of the least". At the opening an illuminated Address was presented to Dr Muir:

> We feel we cannot allow the opening of the TC to pass without a word of heartfelt recognition of all that it owes to you. The inspiration of the work was entirely due to a speech of your own in the Town Hall of Grahamstown in 1894. Amid many failures we can honestly say that we have tried to follow out the high ideal of character-training set forth in your speech on Degree Day 1900. Our earnest hope is that the

students of the TC, by learning to be honest and truthful, courteous and unselfish; to be ready to help the weakest, and to learn from the meanest, to recognise true nobleness, and goodness, and to pay respect to it, in whatever guise it may be found, may be among the rewards of your many years of hard work for our land.

Sisters Eva, Ethel, Clare, Cecile. May 25, 1904

The role of Sisters in the Institution

Mother Cecile died in February 1906 a few days after major surgery. In her place the Sisters elected Sister Florence to be the next Mother and Superior of the Community,

There can be no doubt at all that Mother Cecile was a remarkable person who was outstandingly successful in what she undertook. Qualities which were high-lighted by those who knew and admired her were her spirit of tolerance and her broad view of education, her incomparable charm, her intellectual capacity, her powers of organisation and her sense of humour. She was remembered for her strong character, her staunch faith, her love of fun, her courage and her radiant happiness. Dr Muir recalled her love for everything good and true and beautiful and, above all, her devotion to duty. He summed it up in his remark: "Fortunate is the land which can inspire such devotion and profit by such a life."

Over the years the Community was involved in education through the many schools it established as well as in the training of teachers, but it was particularly through TC that the Community reached out and touched a wide area of life in South Africa. It was this work for which the Community was probably best known. The work which the Sisters did at TC was of a two-fold nature: first, to qualify these teachers professionally; secondly, to form and establish in them those high ideals which in turn would affect the lives of the children they taught.

The Mother Superior of the Community was also the Manager of the College; but her priority was always to the Community. It was her privilege as Superior of the Community to place Sisters wherever and whenever she felt was necessary. The fact that the Sisters were not free to choose their work and could be sent off at little notice was to create problems at TC from time to time.

Not all the women who joined the Community were trained graduate teachers; that was not a requirement of those wishing to join. Nor were they young women straight out of school or college; they were more generally of middle age or even older with perhaps years of experience in their chosen career. Between 1910 and 1929, 54 women were professed into the Community but in that time the work undertaken had also increased. (The work in which the CR was involved included running orphanages, hostels and parish work, in addition to the educational work they established.)

At TC Sisters not only held teaching posts but were also used as Hostel Matrons where they played valuable roles. The residential life of the College was closely linked with the academic work. The Principal and Vice-Principal with the assistance of other members of the Community shared the work of supervising evening study in the classrooms and library; they also did weekend duties. This meant that the students were continually under the influence of the Community, an influence that was to stand them in good stead in later life.

By 1947 the number of Sisters on the staff of TC had declined. A lay member of staff at that time commented that a teaching Sister had a peculiar advantage in that she was more than just an individual. She enjoyed the strong backing of the Community. She was resident and easily available, and she met the students, the majority of whom were resident also, in other than the student-teacher relationship and so learnt to know them as "whole" individuals. For a teaching Sister, teaching was not a matter of the Departmental five-hour day but in addition to her religious duties was an all-time all-absorbing interest. That this was of value was proved by the close contact maintained with the College by old students who later sent their daughters to TC to be trained. This sentiment applied equally to the Hostel Sisters.

In 1908, when it was decided by the Education Department that women would henceforth be eligible for appointment as Principals of Training Colleges, the Education Gazette mentioned that at that point TC with an enrolment of 180 students was entirely controlled by women.

The number of teaching Sisters at TC was of importance, as a reference in the Chapter Minutes regarding finances made clear. Attention was drawn to the fact that at that point it was no longer possible to put salaries into the Building Fund, as those earned by the teaching Sisters at TC had to be used to make up the bigger salaries now paid to the rest of the staff.

By 1946 the College staff consisted of 14 lay members and three teaching Sisters. It was pointed out in a letter to the English Helpers that one could not appeal for Sisters as one did for recruits to the mission field because the religious vocation is entirely a gift from God. The Religious Life was a vocation quite distinct and separate from the call to teaching. The Community needed teaching Sisters above all.

TC was not a money-making undertaking. Throughout its history its expansion and development were hampered by lack of capital. Time and again, money had to be obtained by means of overdrafts at the bank or by loans. Unfortunately, the students were under the impression that the Training College was rich and that the Community was an extremely wealthy "body". In 1932 the Principal took the "bull by the horns" and wrote about the finances in the College Magazine. This was felt to be the best way of clarifying the situation and removing the false impression regarding the financial affairs of the college and it was hoped this would bring about a change in the students' general attitude.

The Music School

In his first report as SGE in 1892 Dr Muir wrote that he had noticed the higher than average natural ability of the people for music but that he was surprised that little was being done in the schools to develop the talent. This seemed to be the norm. South Africa was a country in which people enjoyed music yet few students who had passed the Teachers' Certificate examination were competent to teach vocal music in schools.

The Inspector for the Eastern Districts Circuit reported that, in some schools attempts had been made. He found that singing by note using the sol-fa system was attempted in 84% of the schools he visited. He mentioned that pupils were debarred from singing for one or other of the following reasons: "Because they are Malays; have bad voices; are in the school higher class; have breaking voices; take science; show little capacity; are infants; are very little ones."

Timetables were often at fault and many teachers were careless about the time devoted to singing. In a few of the schools where instruction was given the Inspector reported that the younger children were withdrawn from the lesson because of their youth. They were even debarred from Action Songs. Not surprisingly the staff at the training schools/colleges complained that pupil-teachers beginning training were quite ignorant of the art of singing. According to the Inspector many when they left college were still ignorant where the teaching of singing was concerned!

Mother Cecile had opened St Peter's School in 1884. At the school music featured largely on the daily timetable. Throughout the period from 1885 to 1950 the entire enrolment at the school was instructed in class singing. Singing from notes formed a prominent feature of the curriculum. The syllabus was consistently followed, and reports suggest that a high standard of work was achieved. What Dr Muir and his Inspectors hoped would happen in the Cape Colony was already happening at St Peter's School in Grahamstown under the guidance of the Sisters. The school was a model of what could be done with suitably trained teachers.

What reports were received on music at the Training School in Grahamstown? The Inspectors were not exactly carried away! The Inspector of Vocal Music in 1898 mentioned that two-part voluntaries were well attempted and ear training was satisfactory. The attempt at sight-reading in time and tune was somewhat marred by weakness in the knowledge of time. First- and second-year students devoted one-and-a-half hours per week to singing. Third-year students only spent one hour. The report for 1899 was no better. The inspector considered that the standard reached in music was below that expected from a training school. The candidates were inadequately prepared and there was little evidence that the average student was really qualifying as a teacher of singing. For the teachers in the Training School this was indeed "naught for your comfort"!

The report for the 27 August 1900 was more encouraging. The Inspector noted that the subject had received more attention than in preceding years but that some practice in teaching singing ought to be given. By 1905 the Inspector reported that great attention to detail was being paid and that the singing was superior to that of any former year. He was pleased at the increase in the higher (Music) awards and felt that the institution was doing excellent work the influence of which was being made more and more apparent throughout the Colony.

CHAPTER 3

TC under Sister Clare
1904–1920

SISTER CLARE WAS Principal from 1904 to 1920 and under her guidance the College was well established. She was assisted by Sisters some of whom were to be associated with the College for many years. At first her staff at the College was limited to six or seven other Sisters – but it expanded steadily as student numbers grew and because of the need for subject specialists (e.g. "High Dutch", Music, Drawing) who were often lay staff and not Sisters.

When Sister Clare retired in 1920 the Education Gazette mentioned that she was a teacher known throughout the educational service. She had laboured in the cause of education for over 30 years having been Principal of the Grahamstown TC since 1904. She had filled this position with conspicuous ability and her old students were to be found doing good service in all parts of the province. Hundreds of schools were indebted to her for the work she had done in the training of teachers.

During Sister Clare's time as Principal the College had firmly established itself among the leading educational institutions of the country with the honourable record of having passed out some 2500 students during its existence. TC and Sister Clare were synonymous. It was due to her strong personality, her unfailing devotion to duty, and her great administrative capacity, that the College had achieved its striking success. The progress made can be gauged by reference to the Inspection Reports during her tenure of office.

Early in 1905 it was noted that the progress of preceding years in the TC was more than being maintained that year. The new session had opened with 132 students, 44 more than the previous year. The increase was spread throughout the T3, T2 and Kindergarten (KG) classes. Attention was drawn to the blackboard drawing examination and it was noted that in Grahamstown the work was of a high standard. Candidates presented sound drawing and showed an appreciation of the materials used and of the purpose for which they were used – namely, that of class teaching.

In the 1906 examinations TC was still a front-runner. Of 165 candidates all except seven passed and 59 passed in the first class. 1907 continued along the same lines. The second-year results of the Pupil-Teachers' examinations were exceptional. Grahamstown once again took first place among the European training schools with 16 firsts and 27 seconds out of 52 candidates. The third-year results were equally satisfactory.

In both 1909 and again in 1913 reference was made in reports to Reading and Recitation. As a subject, recitation required much individual treatment if each student's faults of pronunciation and diction were to be corrected. TC was recognised as an institution where the careful teaching of reading and recitation produced good results with a high standard of pronunciation and voice production. The students were taught to use the voice with a pure full tone.

The Inspection of July–August 1917 once again congratulated the College on the constant efforts which were made to improve the students' speech in clarity and accuracy. It was also remarked that literary study in the college was on liberal intelligent lines thus increasing the students' personal culture and breadth of interest.

All this teaching was being conducted in classrooms which were described as large, well-ventilated, and well equipped for their purpose. There were excellent framed pictures on the walls in the corridors and classrooms. The classes were well organised, and the work fairly apportioned among the staff according to ability and special qualifications. The tone and discipline of the College were described as excellent and the students were described as growing in refinement of character and in general culture with each year of residence.

In Class Teaching it was clear that the utmost pains had been taken by the staff in training the pupil-teachers to use good methods and to use them with intelligence. The importance of good black-board work was dinned into the students at TC from the start of their course. The report for 1917 also drew attention to the fact that the class teaching was of exceptionally good quality as was also the Drill and Drawing, Elocution and Reading.

As early as 1905 the discipline and tone of the College were seen to be of a high standard and the earnestness of the staff and the students was exemplary. The College fully maintained its high reputation for hard and thorough work and much credit was due to the staff. A notable feature of TC was the effort to make the courses of training not merely professionally effective but also a contribution towards the students' overall personal development. The class-reading for instance was a real initiation into the pleasures of literature to which many of the students were strangers when they entered the College. The exercises in elocution introduced the students not only to the older classics but also to much fine contemporary work. Good taste was further cultivated among the students by playing and listening to good music.

The Annual Inspection in 1919 was in May which was uncomfortably early in the year. Nonetheless it was reported that the work in practical subjects was not only well advanced but that in many areas a level of proficiency had been attained which would be remarkable even at the end of the year. The Inspectors considered that the students who qualified at TC would not only be effective and conscientious teachers but would possess a breadth of interest and refinement of taste which would make them valuable members of the communities they served. The average age of students in training as pupil-teachers was sixteen years and six months towards the end of the first year. They went out to teach in the schools before the age of nineteen.

Already in 1919 just before the entry standard was raised to the Junior Certificate level, Sister Clare had written of the decision taken by the staff to consult the prefects more and more as occasion arose. It was also felt by the Sisters and the staff that the innovation of giving the "girls" a general voice in the choosing of their prefects was a move justified by the result. At the end of each year all the students voted for the prefects for the coming year. The staff would then consider the list of girls who had received a fair number of votes. As a rule, the staff confirmed the choice made by the girls.

The staff recognised that the students were now a bit older than previously and that as they were intending to be teachers they must be given some freedom. All was not perfect, as Sister Clare admitted. The staff was experiencing difficulties where discipline was concerned. In her report of 29 November 1918 Sister Clare had noted that there was considerable insubordination among the first-year students evident particularly during September. There were petty incidents. These had become frequent and difficult to deal with; and there had been rudeness and disobedience to teachers. She felt the matter required a resolution in view of the changing status of women as citizens.

Sister Clare and her staff had laboured long and hard and the foundations had been well laid. From small beginnings TC had grown to be one of the largest, best organised and most efficient centres of training in South Africa. Sister Clare though had both feet on the ground and was aware of weaknesses within the College. Her comments on the candidates for the examinations in 1920 are revealing: "...expect many failures. There is a very long and limp 'tail' in each of these classes, and it will be a thousand pities if such derelicts are passed. It is painful to have failures, but it is worse to push into the teaching profession candidates who are fundamentally unfit to bear responsibility owing to slackness of mental and moral fibre." Of the 186 entered, 167 passed!

In their Annual Letter in 1920 members of the Old Girls' Guild wrote this about Sister Clare: "In a land where it is uphill work to secure the best conditions for education, we have had, largely through her endeavour, the help of beautiful grounds, of music, pictures and books. Above all, we have had her own exhilarating personality. She knew us well, our little weaknesses as well as our good points. Her praise was generously given where she saw improvement, and so wisely that it spurred one on to reach a still higher standard."

The Bishop said, "I am quite sure that none of the OGs can ever forget Sister Clare and the work that she did for so many years, the tremendous vigour that she put into everything, her great intellectual power, all of which not only very largely made the College what it is today but set a standard for all members of the Training College in the future. We know that we have been in touch with one whose thoroughness and stimulating power we shall rarely, if ever, see equalled."

Sister Clare was a teacher for 35 years, 30 of them in Grahamstown where she arrived in 1891. She taught first at St Peter's School, then at the Training School as Vice-Principal under Mr Rankin in 1900, and then Principal from 1904. Another side of Sister Clare known only to those who had served on the Board was her exceptional efficiency. At their meetings the Board members were always deeply impressed with the results of such perfect administration and such remarkable management.

Mabel Wood (m. Duncan-Brown) a foundation student, expressed the opinion that it was Sister Clare's tireless energy, discipline and driving force which carried the day. She was the centre of the Training School. It was common talk that she could "twist Dr Thomas Muir around her little finger"! Every request was granted. He had the greatest admiration for her organising capacity and her ability and was as proud as she was when the School (later College) was soundly established.

It is understandable then that the retirement of Sister Clare was viewed with serious regret by the Education Department. It was left to Sister Clare's successor to implement the new regulations pertaining to the training of teachers as follows: a pass in the Junior Certificate Examination of the University of South Africa, or in the new examination which the Department expected to conduct in 1921, would be required for admission to the Lower Primary Teachers' Course in 1922; that course would take only two years. For the Higher Primary Teachers' Certificate, Standard X or a Matriculation Certificate was required on entry. By 1923 the number of students at TC holding the Matric Certificate had risen from 40 to 75. All Primary Teachers were required to take the entire two-year course at a training institution.

After her retirement as Principal of TC Sister Clare withdrew from the Community and as Miss Clare Goodlatte went to live in District Six in Cape Town. Here according to Baruch Hirson in an article entitled: "The Trotskyist Groups in South Africa: A Retrospective View", she became involved with such a group. He wrote: I learnt in the 1940s that there had been a one-time nun in the leadership of the Workers' Party of South Africa. But no details were available, even though she had died (as I found later) in 1942. He added later: in a deserted house in Cape Town, once the residence of Clare Goodlatte, a box of documents was found in the early 1980s. There is still a mystery surrounding this discovery...

Bilingualism at TC

Sister Clare was conscious that Dutch, the second language, required concentrated attention. The Prime Minister, Mr Merriman, had spoken of the need for every English speaker to learn Dutch and for every Dutch speaker to learn English. In many districts of the country teachers were frequently required to speak Dutch and so it was always a desirable attainment for a teacher to be bilingual. Sister Clare noted that the unilingual, certificated teacher would not be eligible for the Good Service Allowance or a Pension.

In 1908 it was made a requirement at TC that all students were to learn Dutch so that the majority could go out able at least to read a Dutch book and to carry on a simple conversation. This objective was one which Sister Clare promoted zealously throughout her time as Principal.

The students were given opportunities to speak the language at the debating society; while every week a dozen students prepared model lessons in Dutch and the criticism of these lessons afterwards was also given in Dutch. Every pupil-teacher had three hours a week of hearing how a lesson was presented through the medium of Dutch. Each student was required to read one Dutch book during the year.

It was clear that the educational authorities were determined to provide teachers who were willing and able to make the effort to master both languages. Sister Clare acknowledged that it was going to be a difficult challenge indeed for the young teachers of English-speaking districts to acquire the bilingual qualification. The tests proposed would be searching and would certainly lie beyond the grasp of the indifferent and the ill-prepared.

The methods employed at TC to ensure proficiency in the second language are worth noting, for there was the added problem in Grahamstown that at least 95% of the European population spoke English and among the large number of school-going children in Grahamstown there were few who spoke Dutch. Sister Clare managed to collect a class of children who not only learnt and spoke Dutch but who would also serve as a model class. Besides this, the first-year pupil-teachers served as practising classes for the seniors. Dutch evenings were introduced and took one of three forms: Lectures when someone from the town was asked to give a lecture in Dutch; debates; or speeches. The log book records in 1917 that on 17 February we had about a dozen little Dutch speeches, some very good, some very bad; and on 24 February we had a debate: *Dat Jongens ondeugender zijn dan Meisjes.* [That boys are more mischievous than girls.] These Dutch speech evenings were found to be most useful.

In 1919 a searching oral examination in Dutch reading and conversation, elocution and class teaching had been conducted and for the first time the marking of English and Dutch was carried out to a uniform standard throughout the Cape Province. The language issue was further complicated by the fact that the High Dutch taught in schools differed greatly from the Cape Dutch or Afrikaans, which was the spoken Dutch of the country.

Sister Kate was to carry on where Sister Clare left off except that by then Afrikaans was the second language throughout TC as it had been decided to substitute Afrikaans for Dutch in the preliminary year of Lower Primary and Higher Primary courses.

The Afrikaans Inspection on 12 November 1924 considered that the study of Afrikaans had been undertaken in exactly the right way by both staff and students and they were commended on the energy, enthusiasm, and ability displayed. The students were prepared by systematic Direct Method lessons on all topics of ordinary conversation throughout the two years of their training.

Extending the Campus

The teaching block

The new block completed in 1904 comprised the T2 and KG rooms and Principal's Office facing Grey Street and one large room at the back divided by moveable partitions into three classrooms. The College Building designed by Mr White-Cooper was officially opened on 25 May 1904. The contract was carried out by Mr GT Weeks. No sooner had the building been brought into use than a further appeal was launched. The building was too small as Dr Muir had predicted at the opening. Dr Muir was not in favour of "additions"; he liked a building to be planned and completed all at once. Much of the charm of the TC campus was that it was developed, and buildings were added as the need arose. It gradually moulded itself into a beautiful setting. The number of students increased so rapidly that an additional five classrooms were urgently needed, and more boarding accommodation was also required. It was this steady growth that put the seal on TC. This observation by Sister Clare sums up what was happening: "There could be no better testimony to the strengths and solidity of Mother Cecile's work than the steady, substantial growth of the institution she founded."

Mother Cecile wrote yet another "begging" letter to the English Helpers' Union (EHU). She pointed out that Dr Muir could not issue building grants to any institution which was not strictly un-denominational, and hence the money for building had to be obtained from some other source. What was proposed was an extra classroom. She wrote that the rough plan and estimate showed that a sum of about £700 would be needed. The money should be in hand by October 1905 to have the new room ready for use by 1 February 1906.

In 1905 Mother Cecile returned to England yet again in search of more money. She was already ill but nothing daunted threw herself into the work of raising money. Annual Meetings of the EHU were held in London and high-profile public figures were called upon to address the meetings to appeal for financial assistance for the TC. For instance, the meeting in December 1903 was chaired by the Bishop of St Andrew's, Bishop Wilkinson; another speaker was Canon Scott Holland. They had both attended the laying of the Foundation Stone of the Teaching Block in August that year. Their speeches were extremely persuasive and emotive. The Bishop worked on the guilt feelings of the English conscience towards South Africa following the War. He spoke of "those silent graves through which you pass as you go up the country from place to place." Canon Scott Holland emphasised the privilege of having a part in the rebuilding of a shattered land, by contributing to the wonderful work being done by the Sisters.

Sister Charlotte Emily added her appeal in a letter to the EHU in mid-1905 pointing out that the College needed to expand and unless they could provide for a large and comprehensive extension within the next five years the growth of this important work would be stifled. The vision was there.

It was the wherewithal that was lacking.

Dr Muir wrote in support of the appeal that if those who had the bestowal of funds knew the history of education in South Africa during the previous 12 years – the continual shortage of teachers of all grades, the need for trained teachers, and the growth from nothing of so excellent a source of supply as TC – he was certain that they would see the need to help. He was anxious to reassure potential givers that there was nothing speculative about the establishment of TC. On the contrary it was an assured success – in fact it was so successful that they were in the embarrassing situation that without increased accommodation students would have to be refused.

The Rev. Douglas Ellison, Warden to the Sisters, pointed out that South African church people had done their part. But it was unlikely that there would be much help forthcoming towards the present undertaking. That was because the Sisters were obliged to make constant appeals to the local generosity and goodwill for additional buildings for the orphans. South Africa was still in a period of great financial depression; and Grahamstown was not one of its wealthier centres.

In December 1905 there was a meeting at the Mansion House in London with the Lord Mayor in the Chair. Among others, the Archbishop of Canterbury was present. As an outcome of all these meetings £9500 was raised. This enabled a large classroom with the Library below to be completed and in 1906 a further five classrooms added to the teaching block of 1904. This improvement meant that the old T2 room could become a Staff Room. Before that the staff had waited about in passages or in empty classrooms.

Mother Cecile had already acknowledged the help received from the EHU: "We have much already for which we are indebted to you in England, and now we have again to look to you as we realise the pressure of the needs. We are doing our utmost to build up the Church of Christ through these young teachers, and we ask you, the friends who have not failed us in the past, to stand by us still." The needs of the teaching side of TC had for the time being been met. Now funds were urgently needed for residential accommodation.

Canterbury House 1907

Mother Cecile died in February 1906. The last fund-raising venture on which she was engaged had been to secure money for a new Hostel for TC. This she managed to achieve with much help from the Archbishop of Canterbury, Randall Thomas Davidson. She received the first disbursement from the fund that the Archbishop had set up to advance the cause of education in South Africa. It was probably the first time in history that an English Archbishop had made such an effort on behalf of a daughter church in the far places of the Empire. The Archbishop donated £4000 to TC. The new Hostel was to bear the name 'Canterbury House' in recognition of this. The House, a most pleasing building, was built on the corner of Grey and Somerset Streets. In the then Common Room above the fireplace was a brass plaque with the words:

AMDG
Randall Thomas
Lord Archbishop of Canterbury
with large hearted care for South Africa and zeal for
Christian education made provision for the building of this House.
July 18th 1907

Do you who dwell herein cherish a grateful remembrance,
not less enduring than these walls, alike of the gift and the giver.
"Bring my sons from far and my daughters from the ends of the earth."

The Common Room was the *pièce de résistance* of the beautiful building. *Grocott's Penny Mail* described it as bringing back memories of old country houses in far-off England with a delightful inglenook around the red-tiled hearth, comfortable wide seats with high backs. At the main entrance the door was approached by a tiled porch with pillars of stone. The door was of teak. The building was designed by Baker and Massey who had come to the rescue at a critical moment as the Community's old and kind friend Mr White-Cooper was ill. The building work had been carried out by Mr James Davidson of Grahamstown.

All was in hand for students to move in to Canterbury House when a fire broke out and the entire roof was destroyed and the first and second floors were severely damaged. At 3.45 p.m. on Friday 12 July, 1907, as reported in *Grocott's Penny Mail*, fire broke out on the top floor. Efforts to extinguish the fire were severely handicapped owing to the lack of any pressure of water.

The contractor Mr Davidson bore the brunt of the financial cost resulting from the fire as the building had not yet been taken over from his company by the Training College authorities. The fire delayed the opening which eventually took place on 2 November 1907.

The next challenge would be to ensure that all accommodation at the College was of the same standard as that of Canterbury. Canterbury House accommodated 60 girls; the rest of the 200 students were lodged elsewhere, for the most part under conditions which left much to be desired. What was needed was a group of permanent buildings worthy of the College and of Mother Cecile's life spent in its service. At TC it was a case of making haste slowly. The College was attempting to hold its own against the better-funded state institutions which were able to draw for their building needs on the public purse. As already seen, fund-raising undertaken by TC depended largely on voluntary effort. The list of buildings that were still required at TC included a College Hall, a suitable Chapel, two more well-equipped boarding houses, a Music School and a well-planned central drainage scheme.

The Mother Cecile Memorial Hall 1909

Immediately after the death of Mother Cecile, plans were put in place to start the Mother Cecile Memorial Fund to commemorate a woman whose life and work had been devoted to binding together the different peoples comprising the emerging South African nation. Money poured in and within a short time the fund stood at £2947 15s 4d. The target was initially set at £4600. This money was to be used to build the Mother Cecile Memorial Hall suitable for the College dining hall and adaptable for a concert hall.

What resulted was a Hall worthy of any Oxford College. It was designed by Baker, Massey and Kendal. It has a steeply inclined roof which is covered with shingles consisting of small blocks of wood cut from Californian red cedar. The construction and materials ensured that the temperature inside the building would be kept constant. Massive jarrah beams specially imported from Australia were used with pleasing and harmonious effect. The windows glazed with leaded-lights give a fine sense of proportion to the building. The Hall is panelled in dark wood with a gallery around three sides of half the Hall, opposite to the "stage" or raised dais at one end. It seated 250 students for meals and was capable of seating 700 for concerts.

The Hall was officially opened on 28 July 1909 by Sir William Solomon. In the end £6559.15.8 was spent on the building. Before the opening of the Memorial Hall students were distributed for meals in three separate buildings: the Barracks, the Bungalow and the Cookery school, where the tables were narrow and the space over-crowded. The Barracks was a plain brick building which after 1909 was used for cubicles. It was demolished in 1913, to be replaced by a new hostel, Lincoln House. The Bungalow was a large wood-and-iron shed bought at a sale of war material. After the completion of the new Hall it was used as a Common Room for girls who were boarding at St Peter's Home and later it was moved to make way for the College Chapel.

The Memorial Hall was a fine addition to the TC's buildings. It had one serious flaw: the kitchen was on the lower level, which meant that food prepared for the students had to be taken to the hall above by way of a "dumb waiter" or "driver lifts". The food was then placed on warming trays or in the bain-marie to be kept warm until eaten. It was only in 1957 that this fault was corrected, and the kitchen moved to the same level as the Hall, replacing what had initially been described as a "retiring room".

Lincoln and Westminster

At the end of 1912 another block was added to the College buildings. This building was paid for partly by setting aside the balance of the salaries of Sisters working at the College and partly by money received from the EHU. Lincoln and Westminster were two boarding houses in a single large building divided in two and able together to accommodate seventy students. This is today known as "Lincoln Inn" and is occupied by the Law Department of Rhodes University. The Superior at the time was Mother Florence and as she was born and grew up in the historic English city of Lincoln the house was so-named. Westminster was named in honour of the then Warden the Rev Francis Phelps (later to be Dean, then Bishop, of Grahamstown, and subsequently Archbishop of Cape Town). He had spent a curacy in the parish of Westminster and had happy memories of the time he spent there.

The Chapel of St Mary and All the Angels

The Chapel was central to the life of the College. From the early days St Peter's Chapel (now referred to as the "Nuns' Chapel") had been used by both the Community and the students. But the College had grown rapidly, and the Chapel was too small for the whole College to worship together. It became necessary to duplicate services. As early as 1911 talk of a Chapel for the College was in the air. The OGG came on board with great alacrity. In their Newsletter for 1912 an appeal was launched but it was decided that no bazaars, concerts or theatricals should be held and no buying or selling methods used to gain money for this fund; the Chapel was to be "a house of prayer, raised by prayer." What was envisaged was a place where it would be possible for the whole College to worship together at least once a week thus allowing the original Chapel to be at all times a house of prayer for the Community.

A Day of Prayer was held, the intention being donations towards the fund. By January 1915 the Chapel Fund stood at £5000; donations were received from friends in England, the OGs and others. The First World War had brought with it its own demands but nevertheless the project of building the Chapel was to go ahead. It would in any case offer employment to those out of work.

The Foundation Stone was laid by the Governor-General, Lord Buxton, on 2 June 1915. This was his first visit to Grahamstown and he came for the express purpose of laying the Stone. In his speech on the occasion Lord Buxton referred to Mother Cecile: "... We know quite well that the Spirit which animated (her) has been continued, and that you girls have the advantage of knowing that behind the work of this school lies the great spirit of education and of religion, and that those who are now occupied in teaching here are animated by that same feeling and that same spirit." The Foundation Stone is inscribed:

> To the Glory of God
> This Foundation Stone was laid by
> H.E. Viscount Buxton
> Governor General
> June 2nd 1915
> "My House shall be the House of Prayer"

In his welcoming address Judge-President Mr Justice Thomas Graham spoke of the noble buildings, the spacious gardens and the throngs of students which were all monuments to the great work which Mother Cecile had begun, and which had been continued on the lines she laid down by a band of noble and devoted Sisters. He concluded his speech by saying that the good seed which was planted by Mother Cecile had grown into a mighty tree and its branches were spreading and those present were witnesses to a new development of the spiritual side of the work which Mother Cecile began.

The Chapel of St Mary and All the Angels was duly consecrated on 14 October 1916. When the College was sold to Rhodes University in 1975, the Sisters of the Community excluded the Chapel from the Deed of Sale. Instead they presented it as a gift to the University to be used as a place of worship by all students. Chapter Minutes for 7 January 1973 record a special clause in the Deed of Sale: "It is a special condition of the Agreement that the Chapel shall remain as a centre for Christian Religious Worship for all denominations; the structure and interior fixtures and fittings shall be maintained by the purchaser in the same good order and repair as at present. The nature of the activities conducted in and the use made of the Chapel shall be under the general surveillance of a Committee [to include the Dean of the Faculty of Theology and the Bishop of Grahamstown] ... In the event of circumstances arising in which the exclusive use of the Chapel for religious purposes is no longer suitable or desirable, the building may, in the sole discretion of the said Bishop of Grahamstown,... be deconsecrated."

As Astrid Anderson wrote in her Chapel Note in the College Magazine in 1957, "In the rush and turmoil of College life, one always finds refreshing peace and quiet in the Chapel around which so much of our College life revolves. The beauty of our 'Sanctuary' leaves a lasting impression on most students who worship in it during their life at College."

The Chapel building is in the Byzantine style, after the fashion of Italian architecture and was constructed from brick with a stucco exterior, the plinths being of rough-hewn stone with a tiled roof. In one corner is a Campanile; and at the other end of the building is the apse for the Sanctuary and Altar. The Chapel can seat 400 to 500 worshippers. The architects were Baker and Kendal of Cape Town; the builders were Messrs Carr and Co, and the Clerk of Works was Mr Preston. TC was indeed unique in South Africa; no other College had a chapel like the Chapel of St Mary and All the Angels occupying the centre of its life; and no other College had a Founder of such rare vision and arresting character as Mother Cecile.

In the apse or half-dome above the altar there were originally four narrow elongated windows. These were out of character with the apse and they took the eye away from the altar. Father Noel SSJE who had been an architect before his ordination, recommended that the windows be filled in and the wall plastered over with a fine finish. Fr Noel then made a further suggestion: that a fresco should be painted in the half-dome.

The fresco in the apse

Sister Margaret, a member of the Community in Grahamstown who was a trained artist, was then put to work. She had been a student of Mr Frampton in London with whom she took a course in fresco painting including the making of the spirit-fresco medium. Painting on a curved surface is a particularly exacting art-form. Sister Margaret records: "My instructor had said, 'Once you have a trustworthy outline, keep to it, and paint inside. Do not try to change it high up on the wall.'" Sister Margaret painted the apse between 1924 and 1929 using students and others as models; it was the result of much prayer and devotion and has been a source of inspiration to many. It was dedicated on 2 February 1929 by the Warden of the Community, the Revd Mr Thornley.

The dedication of the Chapel and the subject of the fresco, St Mary and All the Angels, was chosen by Bishop Phelps who previously had been Warden to the Community. During a visit to Assisi he was attracted by the title of the little chapel where the Franciscan Order had its beginning. There is a legend that St Francis heard angels singing there one night when it was empty and uncared for and named it the "Chapel of St Mary and All Angels" and spared no pains in making it a fitting place of worship.

In the Introduction to his book, "The Prophetic Nun", Guy Butler noted: "Sister Margaret's fresco of St Mary and All the Angels is, by any standards, worth more than passing attention. The subject may not appeal to all, nor will the 'high' Anglo-Catholic mystique, and the style is old-fashioned, but it and subsequent works by her have a prophetic dimension."

The Music School

Where music education was concerned, the tide did eventually turn. The foundations were carefully and laboriously being laid by Mr Deane FRCO. He was associated with TC for sixteen years. In 1893 he conducted weekly choir practices aimed at improving the Chapel services. From 1894 on, Mr Deane took charge of one or two promising students and, as seen from the Inspectors' Reports, improvement slowly followed. By 1904 music in the College was on firmer ground. In that year the Music School was officially inaugurated and over the years was responsible for training many full-time music teachers. Even by then the effect of teaching good music in the government schools was evident. Dr Muir wished to bring good music within the reach of many children in the lonelier districts of the Cape Colony. He believed that this could be achieved by the systematic training in good music of those training to be teachers.

The TC Magazine records how difficult it was in the early years to get together even one or two performers for a musical evening but eventually the general level was much improved. Over the next few years the results of music examinations were encouraging and gradually the number of those learning instruments increased. Since 1904 there had been great improvement but undoubtedly the way for the notable advance had been prepared by the thorough foundation patiently laid by Mr Deane and carefully built upon by him and his colleagues.

Mr Deane had become widely known as a brilliant and most accomplished organist as well as a fine teacher of piano and organ. In 1905 he received a rare distinction. He was made a Fellow of the Royal College of Organists (FRCO) without his having to be present to play in England and without any further test of his powers than that afforded by the uniformly good results of his work as a musician and teacher of music during the previous 15 years. He left TC in 1909 to move to Johannesburg.

The Log Book records that in 1906 there were 173 Music pupils under instruction in Piano and their teachers were Mr Deane, Sister Agnes, Sister Emily, Miss Loudon, Misses Kulling, Franklin and Lawrence. There were 21 Violin pupils, taught by Herr Israel, Mrs Streatfeild and Sister Emily, and 18 Singing pupils who received instruction from Mr Streatfeild and Mrs Krause. The College entered candidates for the Solo Singing examination for the first time in 1906.

The year 1906 was an *annus mirabilis* for TC. Musical Concerts and Musical evenings became a regular feature of life in the College. A dream had been realised. The College Orchestra had been established and was flourishing thanks to the efforts of Mr and Mrs Deane who had ably, kindly and untiringly worked on its behalf. The School of Music had taken off.

The reports of the Inspectors now took on a new note. The Inspector of Singing wrote that the high standard referred to in former reports had been surpassed. The influence which TC students had over music in schools throughout the country had been noticed. It was a valuable contribution. TC-trained teachers were carrying the love of singing and of music into schools the length and breadth of the land. They went out to make music and to enable others to do so too. It was thus acknowledged that the general level of attainment at TC was much higher than formerly.

Musical evenings and recitals followed in rapid succession. The first violin recital ever given by a College student took place on 9 December 1907 with Miss Violet Fergus as soloist.

At the end of the first term in 1908, Mr and Mrs Streatfeild and their pupils presented a Concert. Miss Kathleen Adams gave her first piano recital which was well received. The Mother Cecile Memorial Hall was the ideal venue for these occasions to which people from the town were invited. The Editor of the College Magazine noted in the September 1908 edition that "Music in Grahamstown is showing so marked an upward tendency and the subject is taking so large a place nowadays in the life of the College that it seems necessary to allow it a separate article (in the magazine)."

Results were now received regularly for the various branches of musical tuition: Advanced Piano, Intermediate Piano, Lower Piano, Advanced Violin, Intermediate Singing, Higher Singing, Intermediate Harmony, Higher Harmony and Lower Harmony. There were also classes in the History of Music, on Musical Form, Dictation and Ear Tests to be taught by Mr Percy Ould ARAM who joined the staff at that time. Deborah Woolf writing in the Magazine after an OGs' reunion in December 1908 in which the students had presented a concert considered that "the standard of music at the College is now so high that we are no longer satisfied with anything but the best. This was one of the most enjoyable of the many good concerts we have had this year."

In 1908 there were several innovations. The Singing Inspection took the form of a "little concert" to which the public was admitted. The seven songs already prepared for the Inspector were augmented by instrumental items and included the orchestra, and Mr Farrington the Inspector was asked to sing. The string quartet performed for the first time. This was described as "a delightful experience"; and the trio – piano, violin and 'cello – an entirely new feature in a College programme, excited great interest.

The Training College was able to boast some extremely capable and advanced musicians. Clearly the general standard of the School of Music was being pushed up, dictated largely by the requirements of the University Music Examiners. The Teachers' Diploma Examination was to give way to the University Licentiate in Music. This in turn necessitated additional staff and an extension of the Music School.

In 1909 TC entered one candidate, Miss Violet Fergus, in the newly instituted examination for Licentiates in music. She passed and thus became Grahamstown's first Licentiate and South Africa's first Violin Licentiate. Mr Deane and Herr Israel left the College and Mr Percy Ould was appointed the first Musical Director of the School of Music.

The College was extremely grateful for the entertainment provided by the regular concerts. The orchestra was also congratulated on its sound and steady progress. The Sisters involved in the orchestra were Sisters Mary Joyce and Katherine Maud – violas; Sister Innes – 'cello; and Sister Agnes – double bass. At the OG Reunion in 1910 Mabel Cotton mentioned that "in my days the orchestra was very small and being a member of it I know that every member did not always play in tune; now the standard of the orchestra is very much higher, as is the standard of music in the other departments."

The students who performed in these students' concerts were not just the full-time music students. Some of them were third-year pupil-teachers who found the time to play in the orchestra and sometimes even to contribute solos. It is important to note that all students learnt class singing and that the unison and part songs were sung by the whole student body. In 1912 the orchestra numbered 21 instrumentalists with Mr Percy Ould as the Conductor. A perennial problem where the Orchestra was concerned was the fact that senior students on completion of their training went out into the work place and their places had to be filled again. Mr Ould and his staff were most conscientious and so the tradition was built up and the orchestra came to be an indispensable and ever-popular part of the programmes of musical events.

In 1912 there were some astounding results in the various music examinations. Katie van Reenen, at 15 years of age, passed Advanced Harmony and Advanced Piano, obtaining in the latter subject 146 marks out of 150, and having on her paper of marks the endorsements: "All excellent" and "Excellent indeed". She was a pupil of Mr Percy Ould. The crowning glory as announced at Prize Giving was the success of three Licentiates who had also been working under Mr Percy Ould, in Piano and Harmony.

Word was spreading and the regular concerts at TC were well subscribed. The Magazine records that at the concert on 1 March the hall was "filled with an attentive and interested audience." Then tragedy struck. Mr Percy Ould died aged 45 on 13 December 1913. He had made a major contribution to the Music School. The orchestra continued under the leadership of Mr Douglas Taylor FRCO, ARCM.

The Log Book records the arrival in Grahamstown on 18 July 1914 of Mr George Wilby. He was in every way a most admirable musician, a fine player, a successful teacher and a good conductor. He was appointed Director of the School of Music and professor of Violin at a salary of £300 per annum. Mr Wilby's first impressions of Grahamstown make interesting reading: "Grahamstown seemed at first a haven of rest. I was soon disillusioned, for I find a power at this Training College of ours, urging on and inducing continuous effort and permeating the whole institution. In England, I was told that South Africans are slackers; I see no signs of it here. The musical standard is an exceptionally high one, evidently the result of the fine teaching available. The response I have had from nearly all my pupils has impressed me considerably." He stressed how necessary it was for the teacher to have a real love for her subject. She had first to get to the heart of her music; then to the heart of her pupil. Under Mr Wilby things really began to hum. He must have been a dynamic personality.

The new Director was keen to develop different kinds of ensemble work. The orchestra was to have two practices every week which would enable it to be more adventurous and tackle more important compositions than previously. The quintet and the quartet were also meeting for a regular weekly practice and other ensemble work was making progress. This meant that the benefit to the students was incalculable, as they became acquainted with the works of great composers in a thorough and intimate way. This was only possible when such special provision was made under the guidance of a Director of wide experience. The orchestra now numbered 23 members.

Private musical evenings were introduced. These were not open to an audience apart from other performers awaiting their turn to perform. Mr Wilby felt that many young players not yet ready for a public performance gave great pleasure to their hearers by an earnest and capable rendering of a simple piece and greatly benefitted themselves by the experience. The Memorial Hall was used even on those private evenings thereby enabling the performers to face the terrifying isolation of the big platform. They were then astonished to find how much tone they could produce and how well their voices rang out in the free space around them.

On Saturday 8 May 1915 the first Orchestral Concert in the history of the College was presented. The report mentioned that the Hall was crowded, and the music seemed to give great pleasure to the attentive audience. Students in the College were now hearing and studying music on a larger scale than they had ever dreamt of. The Orchestra was then preparing Beethoven's *Eroica* Symphony and Schubert's *Symphony in B minor*, and the ensemble class: Schumann's *Quintet*, Brahms' violin and piano sonatas and the Beethoven *Kreutzer* Sonata.

There was comment in the Magazine that, as far as was known, no other students' orchestra in South Africa was regularly engaged upon such work. The music students were being led by their gifted director into wide and rich fields of musical thought and experience, a source of endless profit and delight not only to themselves in their special study, but also to the many others who shared the ripe fruits of their labour in the delightful evenings and concerts they provided.

The Principal, Sister Clare, recorded in the Log Book for 5 December 1914: "Beethoven's *Eroica* symphony was performed in the hall under the conductorship of Mr George Wilby. Hall crowded; notable enthusiasm." The Magazine was more excited about the performance: "...a day to be ever remembered in the annals of the Training College, for on that day was performed our first symphony (the *Eroica*)." This was undoubtedly a tremendous achievement.

The Music School also included the "run-of-the-mill" student in addition to the brilliant stars. The consensus was however that the music was progressing well. The beginners and the pupils of only fair attainment were doing sound work in a thorough and methodical way.

Mr Wilby considered that TC students were fortunate in having opportunities of hearing and taking part in beautiful music. At the beginning of 1916 he admitted that during the past year there had been successes but also failures. He urged the students to brace themselves for fresh efforts. They should be true to their task: practising scales conscientiously, preparing exercises properly, and working patiently and generally slowly at their solos, to present them in a finished and artistic manner. His approach was so typically that of the Founder, Mother Cecile, namely of doing "the best with what we have". It is significant to note that the emphasis all along was faithfulness to the aim of increasing the musical life of the country through the teachers trained at TC.

The Library and its place in the College

As early as 1894, the SGE in his Report emphasised the importance of each school having a library. The Sisters at the Training School and later the Training College were therefore most anxious to teach the students the use of the library and the importance of encouraging reading. How each of the OGs applied what they had been taught at TC depended largely on the circumstances facing them in the schools where they were placed. Each student leaving the College was conscious of the need for a good library for any school and the importance of teaching and encouraging children to read widely. This was only possible if books were available to be read. It is important therefore to have a clear picture of the role played by the library in the life of the students during their three years of training.

From the outset the Sisters were very anxious that girls in training should be made aware of the place of the library and the importance of music and singing in the life of any school where they might be placed. They also stressed the value of remaining in contact with TC after leaving which is why the place of the OGG in affairs of TC became so important.

This article appeared in the College Magazine for 1905:

> At last we have a room, pretty and pleasant and fairly spacious, to serve as a library. There students will be able to have free access to all reference books, and to make such notes and pursue such investigations as their work requires. It is to be a place of SILENCE, and people who abuse its hospitality will be led to the threshold and bid depart.
>
> Bookshelves run along one side of this room from floor to ceiling; one half devoted to fiction, the other to more solid reading. They are not nearly half full, so if any literary friend is inclined to help us to fill them, it will be a praiseworthy act to send us books. Chambers' new edition of 'The Encyclopaedia of English Literature' is at present the moon I should cry for, if crying were likely to produce it; but modern works of science, books of travel and biographies are all only meagrely represented.

The students were all encouraged to read for recreation and to make full use of reference books. The library was an important place at the College; it was by no means an optional extra! The report following the Annual Inspection in November 1930 mentioned the excellent library and reading room.

Years later, the Departmental Library Organiser on a visit to TC in February 1967 stated that TC library was the best stocked and used of all the College Libraries. She praised the good stock and selection of books and the fact that the library was used as the "workshop" of the college. She congratulated the lecturers at the head of every department who had co-operated and put time and care into the choice of books ordered. The amount to be spent on new books was divided into proportionate amounts for each subject and the lecturer in charge of that subject then chose the books to be ordered.

It is little wonder then that the young women going from the College to postings around the country were anxious to set up little libraries in the schools and ensure their use. For instance, Thelma Gibson writing from Lady Grey mentioned that "every day I thank my mother for sending me to TC, and the Sisters and girls for what they taught me. Many things will be a living memory to me all my life. I have started a small library in my classroom (collected books by borrowing and being given). Every Friday I give books to the children...and they read them during the weekend. All through the week they remind me that on Friday I must give them story books to read. I never have any peace on Monday until they have written a sort of story about the book they took home."

By June 1904 the library already numbered 680 books and the Sister in charge had listed 85 readers. In the Annual Inspection Report for October– November 1909 there is a comment that a wider range of reading in Library has been attempted and the results have been evident both in the students' increased knowledge of English Classics and in their extensive vocabulary.

To begin with books for the library arrived in ones and twos given by well-wishers. By 1908 the library had more books than the shelves could hold. There were plans to relocate the library to a more convenient spot. This continual moving of the library was to be a feature of its existence until the library building was erected and opened in 1940.

The librarian drew attention to the shelf reserved for poetry, biography, history and science and the wide range of classics available. Sister Clare, the Principal, gave the students valuable hints and advice on how and what to read. Her talk aroused an interest in good literature and non-fiction. It was suggested that all leavers should present a book or several books to the library in memory of their time in College

The Dutch language section in the library was launched in 1909 when the long-expected case from Holland arrived containing 30 precious volumes of works by van Lennep, ten Brink, Multatuli, Bosboom-Toussaint, Hildebrand and Justus van Maurik. With the change-over from Dutch to Afrikaans in schools, attention was then turned to Afrikaans books. A cupboard was requisitioned for this purpose.

The OGs were invariably keen to ensure that books were available for their pupils to take home and read. It was expected that the teacher would encourage and instil the habit of reading even though she might have to forego free time. Teachers were encouraged to persevere in teaching good reading and recitation by encouraging good expression and correcting faulty pronunciation.

In the SGE Report for 1905 TC was complimented on the excellent training given in these subjects. This became apparent in the schools where OGs taught. Dr Muir expressed himself with typical Scots bluntness: "It must never be forgotten that the object of a school library is not merely to make the children more intelligent, and therefore, better fitted for their ordinary school work; it is also *to develop a taste for reading and an interest in books.*" From among the school children of the day were to come the friends and managers of the Public Library in the future. The library it was hoped would extend the child's horizon beyond the boundaries of the restricted daily routine of farm life. Progress had been made and thanks were expressed for the initiative of the teachers who in their turn were putting into practice the lessons learnt at the College. There was scarcely anything more valuable to be acquired at school than the importance of a taste for reading.

The Magazine

The Magazine and the Old Girls' Guild both came to be of paramount importance as the years passed. At first from 1904 the Magazine was published quarterly. This was later reduced to twice and then finally once a year. It was helpful to have Sisters available to "put together" each edition without placing added strain on the already pressed members of staff.

The Magazine revived memories of life at College for the OGs. Any official changes in the Curriculum were carefully explained and model lessons were printed in the pages of the Magazine. There were regular sections on the library and the School of Music. Prize Giving and Founder's Day were covered in detail. Sporting activities received attention, and there was a regular Chapel report.

The OGs section is interesting. Not only do we learn of the placements and schools where the newly trained were sent but later, as the admission requirement was raised for teacher training, the growing sophistication of the new teachers is revealed. No longer after the 1930s do we read of experiences in isolated places; then the emphasis was on the beginning of families and the birth of babies. All children of OGs were referred to as "College Babies/Children"!

The Magazine was valued by those who received it and eagerly anticipated. It was a link between the College and the ever-growing scattered family of OGs. Writing to the Principal, a Government inspector mentioned that the fact that TC occupied such a unique position compared with other Training Colleges made the receipt of TC magazines so much more valuable. He felt the magazines recalled the Spirit of the College so full of laughter and yet so charged with the realisation of the responsibilities of life.

An OG wrote that "our magazine keeps us in touch – it does more – it helps us to be more contented with our lives when they have not fallen in pleasant places; in this way if, when we feel a wave of self-pity, we open a magazine and see that one of our companions for instance, took six days to reach her destination; while another lives surrounded by natives, we cannot help feeling that compared with some others we are blessed indeed."

The Magazine was also used as a vehicle for information. For instance, in 1909 a note appeared that "those of you who are learning, or teaching Dutch will find *'Die Unie'* a great help. It is a monthly paper written in the simplified High Dutch which is taught in all schools and containing a great variety of articles of general interest besides detailed information concerning Dutch text books and the *Taalbond* examination."

In her quarterly report to the Advisory Board in 1920 Sister Clare referred to the new Syllabus for Primary Schools. She considered the syllabus to be an interesting one but admitted that it demanded much from the inexperienced 18-year-old teachers isolated on farms, without books or counsellors. Opportunity was taken in the Magazine to publish the detailed syllabus and suggest appropriate books. Some specimen lessons were also provided.

The Magazine was used to answer questions received from OGs where these answers might be of general use. The Magazine for June 1910 mentioned two OGs who wrote of the difficulty of getting children to speak out clearly in reading and recitation. Some useful advice was then offered in the hope that it might be helpful to more than those two OGs. Sister Dora wrote an excellent article for the Magazine entitled: "School Prayers". In her opinion the custom of prayers at school offered an opportunity for the teacher to lead her children in the practice of religion.

The Old Girls' Guild

The inaugural meeting of the OGG took place on Tuesday 2 October 1906 when 16 students joined. It was to be known as the Old Girls Guild or alternately as The Guild of The Resurrection. The aim of the Guild was to "bind together all who have been at the College in order to help and strengthen those who have left and to keep them in touch with the Sisters." In September 1904 Mother Cecile had urged: "I hope that all those who go out from TC, amongst other things will be thoroughly convinced of the Duty of Happiness, making the world, especially their own home, the brighter and the more truly happy by their presence."

The important Reunion of OGs at College began in December 1906. It was not always easy or possible for OGs to attend the annual reunions. Many did make the effort and numbers attending increased as the number of OGs grew. After 1925 the Reunion was held every three years and from 1957 the Reunions coincided with Founder's Day.

One OG wrote: "Of all the links that bind us to College, Reunion is surely the strongest. It is a privilege for which, though we may not always be able to avail ourselves of it, we are nonetheless grateful." She continued: "What shall we say of what Reunion does for us? We know there will be much joy in hearing, one from the other, one-time teacher from former pupil, of some work well done, some progress made, and we should like you to think of us also as fighting the good fight... Whether against loneliness or whatever it be, and striving perhaps more than in past years, to keep polished those corners of God's Temple for which we stand."

Another OG wrote: "I should like to say what the reunion does for me personally, and what I think it will do for all who are able to avail themselves of the kind invitation we receive. We return to our duties full of good resolutions to strive more earnestly and faithfully to perform them in accordance with the ideals of our old College days, and to make the uncongenial bit more congenial by doing all in the spirit that we see pervading everything about our old College, and we find ourselves looking forward to the next reunion with even more pleasure than we had in anticipating the last."

At the Annual Meeting in September 1913 Mother Florence stressed that if an OG wanted to refresh her ideals or seek advice she would always be welcome to visit College for a stay. The OGs appreciated the interest taken in them. They found it a comfort to remember that the College did care for them. Many still needed shepherding and found they could indeed turn to those at the *alma mater.*

Sister Elise was responsible for the OGG and gave unsparing thought and care in her correspondence and in her personal contacts with the OGs. This played a great part in keeping the family sense at TC alive and strong. This readiness to nurture and encourage OGs became a feature of TC. Sister Virginia, the last of the Sisters Principal, was lauded for her willingness to go to great lengths to be of assistance to an OG.

CHAPTER 4

TC under Sister Kate
1921–1931

SISTER KATE WAS the Principal from 1921 to 1931. She was a born teacher who was devoted wholeheartedly to the College and its students. Inspector Anderson considered that in Sister Kate the College would have a splendid head fitted in every way to continue its great tradition and to lead it on to fresh achievements.

These years were a time of readjustment and progress towards a greater freedom and scope for experiment. By inclination and training Sister Kate was an historian and since 1908 she had been undergoing the necessary specialisation for her subsequent work which enabled her to give a remarkably balanced exposition of the Primary School Syllabus. She guided the whole staff in making teaching less a matter of imparting information than one of integrating the various strands of thought and activity which should go to form an educated mind.

Sister Kate was fortunate where her staff was concerned. The informal Inspection in October 1921 stated that the tone of the Institution was excellent. The congenial environment and the good feeling which prevailed between teachers and students could not fail to have a beneficial effect on the students. The expectation was that the high service and influence

44

shown by Sister Clare would continue to an even higher degree under Sister Kate who had a broad and humane view of education.

The students were described as bright and alert and keen to do their work as thoroughly as possible. They benefitted greatly from the cultural influence of the College and the various activities encouraged by the staff (e.g. musical recitals). On the social side there was a strong, healthy *esprit de corps*. The Sisters had always ensured that the physical side of life received attention. Hence sport was an important part of the daily timetable.

Year after year favourable comments emerged from the annual inspection. The members of staff were described as deeply in earnest, thoroughly competent, with a keen sense of duty and responsibility, and were seen to elicit an enthusiastic response from the students. The inspectors commented on the remarkably good exam results achieved without neglecting other aspects of the training. A strong cultural influence, religious, social, and musical, was evident in the life of the College. Something on which great emphasis was placed was the matter of elocution and correct speech and pronunciation. TC had from the outset been a pioneer in voice and speech training.

Amongst the problems that Sister Kate had to face was the Departmental attempt to widen school curricula which made necessary special courses for teachers. It became necessary to introduce courses in Agricultural Nature Study, Domestic Science and Music. Then in 1928 came the information that from 1929 all future entrants to the Primary Teachers' Lower Certificate (PTLC) would require a Matriculation Certificate. The Primary Teachers' Higher Certificate would be an additional one-year course after completion of the PTLC. By the end of 1930 TC had suffered the loss of some fifty students as a direct result of the discontinuation of the old primary lower course. This was a serious consideration for TC as finances were never very healthy.

Grahamstown Training College was in a unique position. It was the largest Training College in the Cape Province. It was owned by the Community but was aided by the Government. The Community through the fees received had to provide half the salaries of the teachers, the other half being furnished by the Department. Teachers were employed on the same footing as those in schools fully maintained by the Department. The strain of meeting Government salaries was proving too much of a financial burden. Repeated applications were submitted to the Department for a reconsideration of this 50-50 arrangement. Finally, after representation had been made to the SGE, the MP for the area and the MPC and then to the Administrator, came the news that as from April 1925 the Department would pay two-thirds of the teachers' salaries.

At about the same time there were dark clouds appearing on the horizon. At the Education Conference held in Pretoria in July 1928 there was a strong consensus in favour of university training for teachers. Teachers themselves were far from unanimous on this question, certainly where the training of primary teachers was concerned. The Cape Education Department had consistently expressed the view that the training of secondary teachers was a matter for university institutions but that the training of primary teachers was a matter for special training colleges. This was yet another problem to land on the desk of the Sister Principal.

Grahamstown Training College was clearly recognised for its worth. The priorities underlying the foundation continued in place. There was something more striking than just educational efficiency; the characters of the students were being deepened, their ideals raised, their contact with God made sure. Speaking at Founder's Day the Archbishop of Cape Town pointed out that Mother Cecile had laid the foundations of the College so wisely that there could be no suspicion applied to this College that piety was made the excuse for inefficiency. Her successors were careful to carry on that standard. Visitors were struck by the atmosphere of TC. They recognised the sense of service and the devotion to duty and high ideals of those involved in the institution.

So many changes had taken place that as the Triennial Reunion of OGs in 1931 approached, the Sisters feared that the OGs would feel the "old place" was not the same. Instead, the OGs left them feeling encouraged and inspired. Ruth Earp, an Old Girl who had attended that Reunion wrote afterwards, "It was so lovely being back at College that I feel I must tell you how we appreciated all you and the Community did for us. There is an indescribable something in the atmosphere of College that one can capture no-where else. Chapel, the beautiful grounds, even the houses themselves, seem to breathe peace and happiness. Whatever it is, I feel I am going back to my work next term to begin with renewed energy and vigour."

Sister Kate relinquished the principalship at the end of 1931 and, like her predecessor Sister Clare, withdrew from the Community, returning to her home village in Lincolnshire. The Training College had certainly benefitted from her leadership. Sister Irene wrote in the College Magazine that the College owed a great deal to the unsparing work that Sister Kate had put into it. She had always set a high ideal of efficiency and devotion to duty before the staff and students. An example of this efficiency may be construed from the following extract from the "Principal's Book" under the heading "Note on Punctuality: It is essential that the Principal should be prompt and punctual on all occasions when she is due to be with students. Nothing should hinder her from prompt attendance when taking meals, evening prayers, morning prayers, and (unless real emergency) lessons for which she is due; in the first two cases she should be in the room or Chapel before the girls come in. It makes for settled order."

Sister Kate was followed as Principal by Sister Frances Mary (1931–1946).

Extensions to Campus during Sister Kate's time as Principal
Bangor House

Bangor House was built to accommodate fifty students who had previously been accommodated in small houses near the College. It was occupied in the first term of 1923. Once again there had been problems finding the money required for this building, the cost of which was estimated at £7350. The College offered various sums on fixed deposit amounting in all to £492-13-6 plus whatever interest had accrued. The Community offered to advance a similar amount and it was hoped there might be help forthcoming from Sisters' salaries. For the rest a loan from the Building Society was envisaged.

Beethoven House (Music School)

The School of Music had been "in" the College in a physical sense, but not "of" it. In the early days members of the music staff were housed in cottages and the practising rooms stretched in two long rows, one near the Kowie Ditch, the other opposite it on the other side of the netball field. In the early 1920s it was decided that a single building to house the School would be an advantage. Rather than build it in stages it was in the end thought best to borrow the money and put up the whole building at once.

In August 1926 the Superior informed the Sisters that the contract (£8000) for the new College building would be signed that week. The amount required was to be met partly by savings, partly by Community capital to be lent to the College at 4%, and partly by an overdraft at the bank.

It had been envisaged that a room on the first floor of the proposed Music block would be used as a drill hall. Miss Poppleton, the Drill Instructress, considered that it would be too small for the purpose as it was too narrow and would not accommodate a full-sized drill class. A special meeting was called to discuss this matter. It was decided that a room of the right shape could easily be obtained by moving the bedrooms intended as boarding accommodation for housekeeping staff.

In the revised plan the whole of the top floor of the new building would be taken up by the drill hall – thus giving a room of 51 ft × 34.6 ft. This was adequate, and it was estimated would add £900 to the cost. It was agreed that the extra money should be spent. The final cost was £8770.12.3. The drill room upstairs was much used not only for drill but also for other forms of entertainment. It had a good height and plenty of light. The floor was of wood blocks and lockers were provided along each side, doubling up as benches.

Beethoven House facing on to Somerset Street was officially opened on Saturday 27 August 1927. Proceedings began with a performance of Beethoven's Overture from *Egmont* and the audience immediately perceived the excellent acoustic properties of the new building. In his speech Sir Thomas Graham mentioned Mr Higgo the Director of the School of Music whose devotion to duty and single-minded interest in the work of the School of Music had raised it to an envied position throughout South Africa. Sir Thomas felt that the future of the School had been assured. Students were being accepted from all parts of South Africa.

After the purchase of the college campus by Rhodes, Beethoven House became the Rhodes Music Department and it has remained so to the present.

School of Music

Mr Wilby retired after ten years at the Music School in 1924. During his tenure the number of music students had grown, and the orchestra had doubled in size. The quarterly concerts had become popular events in the musical life of the city. He was succeeded as Director of the Music School and Conductor of the Orchestra by Mr Archie Higgo.

The following list shows that several music teachers gave long periods of service to the School:
- Miss Gillespie: OG. At TC all her professional life. 1921–1962 (40½ years)
- Mr Walter Dignas: Left in 1967 after approximately 14 years
- Mr Ronald Kirby: 1942–1968. (26 years)
- Mr Iliffe-Higgo: 1920–1952 (32 years)
- Ms Margaret Joyce McCrea: 1938–1975 (38 years)
- Miss Stella Marneweck: 1956, 1960–1975 (16 years)

In October 1928 John Andrews joined the staff as Professor of Music. He was an excellent teacher who set a standard of thorough and intelligent work. He stayed on the staff for six years during which time he advanced the cause of music in every way. There was a true gleefulness about his choirs; and his work with the Choral Society bore its own testimony in public performances to the vigour and delight of its weekly meetings.

The concerts in the Memorial Hall continued to attract excited and enthusiastic audiences. At the concert in March 1927 Schumann's Symphony No 3 in E flat the *Rhenish* was offered. It was probably the first time that it had ever been performed in Grahamstown. The staff at the Music School had set their sights high. The Log Book records what the Principal, Sister Kate, thought of it: "an excellent students' concert, probably the best, all considered, that has ever been given by the College."

It was about this time that the Beethoven Building was opened and for the first time the Music School was housed under one roof. June 1928 saw the Schubert Centenary Concert presented in the Memorial Hall. This included the orchestra, the college choir and soloists. The performance of the *Unfinished* Symphony was of a high quality. The College and the Grahamstown music-going public were being treated to one musical feast after another.

There was an active Music Club in the College which had started in 1924. Over the years it had collected a valuable library of gramophone records. Regular musical evenings and lectures were held. In 1930 the Club procured a new HMV gramophone to replace the old Columbia. The age of "canned music" had arrived. The Music School remained an asset to the College. At the Concert on 22 March 1930, the Orchestra performed the *Jupiter* Symphony by Mozart. Sister "D" noted in the Magazine: "It must have been Mozart who gave such a lovely tone of refinement and sensibility to the evening's enjoyment...one felt that during the whole evening one had been lifted to a higher plane, and that the work being done in the School of Music is beyond an outsider's praise." Then followed in 1931 *Orpheus and Eurydice,* an opera by Gluck; in 1932 Brahms' *Requiem* and *Dido and Aeneas* by Henry Purcell. By then Sister Frances Mary was Principal of TC.

The Old Girls' Guild

In 1925, Sister Kate proposed that local branches of the Guild should be formed in all the big centres of the country. These branches were to be for the mutual encouragement and sympathy between the members and the furtherance of the well-being of the Guild. By March 1926 there was a vigorous branch in East London; by September that year branches had been started in Johannesburg, Cape Town and Queenstown; then followed branches in Grahamstown (1928), and much later in 1947 branches in Cradock, Port Elizabeth, Durban, Umtata, King William's Town and Bloemfontein, when it was agreed unanimously that local branches were to carry on as they were without any formal constitution.

CHAPTER 5

TC under Sister Frances Mary
1931–1946

THE YEAR 1930–1931 brought more changes to the College than any other in its history to that point. Bishop Phelps left Grahamstown after 21 years of close association with TC and of membership of the College Board. Mother Florence retired as Superior after managing the College for 25 years. Sister Dora was allowed a term's extension beyond retiring age but left TC at Easter after about 30 years on the staff. There was the early and unexpected retirement of Sister Kate from the Principalship and the appointment of Sister Frances Mary. Sister Martha for many years senior Housemistress left TC in June on being appointed Novice Mistress by the Superior. Without those giants it seemed at first impossible to continue but the foundations which they had laid so well stood firm.

Numerous changes were to follow in the years to come. What need was there for change? Was it possible to improve on what had been achieved in the past? Sister Frances Mary made quite clear what her attitude to change was and what motivated change. She said that the main aim held good for time and for Eternity but the means for its achievement had to be continually adjusted to the march of contingent circumstances.

TC in the early 1930s

The Inspectors' Report for 1933 mentioned that under the leadership of outstanding women the College had built up a great tradition and the present principal was a worthy successor. She possessed a wide knowledge of modern educational theory and practice and was not afraid to embark on educational experiments. Her grasp of the needs of the Institution combined with her knowledge of each individual student left no doubt that the future of the College was safe under her guidance.

In addition to the Principal, the College was also fortunate in its staff. They were competent and had a high sense of duty which set the tone of the institution. At no time did TC rest on its laurels; there was always a striving after improvement. Sister Frances Mary felt optimistic about the College and its future. She admitted there were times of prosperity and times of chastening in its history, but she reiterated that the optimism did not rest on a material basis. From Mother Cecile on, there was the steady strength of the Community as the foundation rock. Hundreds of OGs retained their special interest in their *alma mater*. The Principal spoke of the loyal and self-spending staff and of the students who had proved zealous and reliable "custodians of the present".

The new Principal

Frances Banks received her training at Cherwell Hall, Oxford. She held the Cambridge Teacher's Certificate 1913, the Bachelor of Arts from London University 1914, and the Master of Arts from Rhodes University College in Psychology 1930. In a reference received on her behalf by the Superior as Manager of the TC, her tutor at Cherwell Hall, wrote of her ability. "While she was reading for her London Degree, Frances Banks studied Psychology and Philosophy with me and I was particularly impressed with her intellectual ability which is of a high order; she showed unusual powers of abstract thought and a vital appreciation of philosophical problems... she has always taken an interest in the various modern branches of philosophical enquiry. She has a sense of humour and of proportion which will prevent her work from becoming stereotyped."

Frances Banks was born in 1892. Writing of her education, she remarked that many girls of her generation had no opportunity of acquiring a qualification and ended up staying at home and "pottering". She herself had acquired a degree and a teaching qualification, depending on these to ensure financial independence and a gateway to further ventures.

After her withdrawal from the Community, Frances Banks recorded that during 25 years as a Sister she had been trained as a Psychologist, had taught and lectured in a training college for women teachers, with 15 years as Principal. She had become something of a specialist in religious education and had taken part in the framing of an Agreed Syllabus for Government Schools

While in charge of the Primary Higher Course at TC Sister Frances Mary developed the teaching of psychology to a level not before known in a training college but afterwards familiar to many from her book *Conduct and Ability* published in 1936. Later as Principal she assumed that students could and should be trained to a large measure of self-government. Among her many contributions to the development of TC were the introduction of Art and Eurhythmics, the annual observance of Founder's Day, and the Monday address at evening prayers. Relations with African Training Colleges of the area were encouraged, and an interchange of visits was begun. She introduced lectures on Educational Principles and started the assignment system.

An extract from the foreword of her broadcast talks gives a good idea of Sister Frances Mary's approach to her task of preparing teachers: "...teachers tend to lose heart concerning the legacy of factual knowledge which they strive to hand on to their children, for even 'facts' are constantly under revision in an unfolding universe. They too must reassert their belief in the greater importance of becoming than of knowing, and of that inner development which opens the channels of awareness, creates right attitudes, and gives a meaning and purpose to life which can overcome circumstances and stand independent of exterior aids."

Matriculation requirement

Shortly before Sister Frances Mary took over from Sister Kate as Principal, the Education Department had decreed that henceforth Matriculation would be the entrance requirement to a teacher training college. Previously the requirement for the Primary Lower Certificate had been the Junior Certificate. From now on the initial training course would be of two years' duration for a Primary Teachers' Certificate. There would be an optional third year of training for the Primary Teachers' Higher Certificate. This would equip the primary teacher as a specialist in some branch of primary school work in addition to the initial training as a "general practitioner".

The language issue and bilingualism

In 1945 further changes involving the language issue were introduced. At TC this matter had received continual attention. In 1933 Sister Frances Mary had noted that the standard of the Higher Grade in both languages continued to rise and that the standard of the Lower Grade was also being raised, making it almost impossible for any student to pass if she had no knowledge of the second language before entering on her course of training. At TC a special class had been arranged for Saturdays to assist such students. Two members of staff even volunteered to take a party of ten students to spend the August holiday weekend at Stone's Hill. It was a great success as no English was spoken from Saturday afternoon to Tuesday morning. Apparently the effect on fluency in Afrikaans was marked.

From 1945 all students who enrolled for the Primary Teachers' Certificate (PTC) were required to pass the teachers' examination in both official languages with at least one on the Higher Grade.

From then on both in the PTC and the HPTC courses the medium of instruction at each college was to be gradually changed by the introduction of the second language as medium so that ultimately equality would be attained in the use of the two languages as media of instruction. Successive Principals of TC found that Grahamstown did not attract Afrikaans-speaking teachers. This Departmental directive created many problems. The requirement of the bilingual certificate also became a serious obstacle and consideration when appointing staff, as for instance in 1934 when Miss Lavinia Gentleman joined TC staff as the Domestic Science Teacher.

The opinion of the staff at TC was that it was a fallacy to believe that dual-medium would lead to greater bilingualism. Those students who arrived at the College already bilingual found that the constant use of Afrikaans was of great benefit.

Domestic Science staff appointments and bilingualism

Grahamstown Training College was asked by the Education Department to start the Domestic Science course in 1930. The Department was anxious that TC should pioneer this work and was confident that the College would make a success of it. The signs were that it would be a popular course. Then Miss Gentleman appeared on the scene. The Principal, by then Sister Frances Mary, had written a letter supporting Miss Gentleman's nomination for the post. Miss Gentleman, who was from Ireland, had already endeavoured to master the second language, even spending a holiday with an Afrikaans-speaking farmer and his family. Sister Frances Mary felt that although Miss Gentleman had not at that date taken the examination she was probably further advanced in the language than the other English-speaking members of staff.

The Education Department was concerned in this matter because this was the only Domestic Science course available at that time at a training college under its authority so the teacher in charge of this course should be bilingual. The Principal felt that the matter of the second language was safeguarded as Miss Bergh who had been assisting with Domestic Science as part of her timetable since 1932 was in fact Afrikaans-speaking. This meant that when she took the class the students were forced to speak Afrikaans and that was also beneficial. Miss Bergh was able to ensure that the students knew the correct Afrikaans terminology demanded of the subject.

The general attitude of the Department was that if a teacher was making a sincere attempt to obtain the Higher Bilingual Certificate it had no hard and fast rule regarding the termination of that teacher's probationary appointment. Miss Gentleman was duly appointed and the Inspection conducted just before her retirement years later in 1950 noted that she had maintained a high standard of work. A thorough foundation had been laid in chemistry and its application to the various branches of Domestic Science. The Inspectors expressed their appreciation of the excellent work done by Miss Gentleman and felt that her retirement was a great loss to education in South Africa.

Assignment method

A Log Book entry for 5 February 1934 notes: "Assignment method: Began with new scheme for private study for which some hours weekly allotted out of college hours to P1, P2, IST [Infant School Teacher]... A remarkable initial sense of study and absorption." TC had launched a completely new scheme for study. The Assignment Method meant that teaching hours were reduced, and timetables had to be re-arranged to allow the students more time to read up on subjects for themselves. This could be done either in classrooms where members of staff were in turn available for coaching and advice or in the reference library. Monthly and quarterly assignments of specific reading or written work were issued in all possible subjects. To get the new system off to a good start the staff had worked in the holidays to have schemes of work ready beforehand and it was later reported that never had a year begun with less loss of time.

There were certain rules accompanying the new system. Assignments were to show certain markers: (IND) which indicated Individual work; where preparation had involved discussion work among a group of students, the completed assignment should be labelled (DIS) with the names of the other members of the group. Group (GW) meant that the assignment had been done by all members of the group either collectively or with each student doing an allotted share. The library was in constant use. It was felt that a deeper spirit of studious absorption pervaded the College. They had cut down the teaching and lecture periods within safe limits but the large range of subjects and especially of practical subjects made it impossible to avoid a large amount of class teaching.

Sister Irene had been responsible for the smooth inauguration of the assignment method of individual work in the College. This new method attracted interest from the other colleges and visitors arrived to see how the method worked. As expected, 1934 was as a result an exceptionally full and busy year but the staff felt that a mile-stone had been achieved.

At the Biennial Inspection the Inspectors showed great interest in the assignment work. Their report as always was of a positive nature. The courses followed, as well as the standard of work in subjects internally examined, were entirely satisfactory although the College did not always restrict itself to the prescribed syllabus. The report following the inspection gave a favourable impression. The College was alive intellectually and the students were kept informed of all modern developments. There was a willingness to embark on new experiments with foresight and skill. Best of all, there was a high idealism in work and conduct which was bound to bear fruit in the schools of the province. It was clearly a strain on both the Principal and the staff to ensure that the standard expected of TC was always maintained.

The College was certainly providing what the SGE considered to be the essential elements in the preparation of teachers. These were first a professional training which would equip the young teachers technically for their work in the schools; secondly a training which would seek to complete their general education especially in those directions where they lacked the necessary knowledge for their teaching; and thirdly the college *milieu* which would provide a suitable environment and opportunities for cultural development (social, artistic and intellectual) and self-education. There was the need for careful individual attention in certain directions which had always been a feature of TC.

Internal assessment

In 1936 a new system was implemented allowing either examinations or assessment. TC chose the latter option. The training colleges were free to frame their own courses and assessments while being subject to some Inspectoral moderation in practical subjects. TC staff aimed to use this liberty to the maximum advantage and to frame a course which would be deeper, more unified and more exciting in its demands upon initiative and thought. The Bilingual examination would be externally examined but each training college would in future assess all students in all subjects by whatever means it found best.

There was to be a Board of Moderators composed of two training college Inspectors and two training college Principals on a rotating basis to ensure consistency of standards. The Certificate would be issued by the

Department. There was a proviso that Bible Knowledge was not to appear with other subjects. Training Colleges were encouraged to frame courses and qualifications in the matter and method of Scripture instruction.

All this involved much work for the Principal and staff as every subject had to be moderated. It also meant a calmer time of continuous work for the students as exams were avoided as far as possible and what counted was the work of the entire course. Being an internal matter meant that a busy fourth term was spent in assessment of the whole two years' work. The Principal reported that with the new approach some of the individual work surpassed anything possible in the old method.

Teaching practice

During 1936 changes were made in arrangements for teaching practice. Departmental Inspectors had requested that students should be given periods of continuous practice in schools. They asked Sister Frances Mary and her staff to reconsider the existing scheme at TC with a view to incorporating some continuous practice and to provide first year students with more opportunities of observing senior students and experienced teachers. It was not possible to provide continuous practice for such a large body of students in Grahamstown and so the staff arranged a week's practice for second year students in their home towns at the beginning of the first quarter. If that was successful, then another week at the beginning of the third quarter would be considered.

Principals of the schools to which TC students were sent were asked to complete reports which would then be submitted to the Department. The students would be expected to keep a record of their teaching. Such a plan would provide more Afrikaans-medium teaching and more practice with Standards IV–VI than was available in Grahamstown. It would also reduce the pressure in term time as the students would no longer require weekly practice periods during some quarters and would be able to concentrate more upon study.

The experiment worked well, and helpful reports were received from Principals. In practically every case the school principal who gave facilities in January expressed willingness to take the same student again. The students too found the experience beneficial. They reported that they appreciated the value of "staff" status; and they realised that the preparation of lessons was a "weighty business". Pupils in the practice schools in Grahamstown had become a little too clear about the difference between a full-time teacher and a teacher who was only a student. Some had become too highly practised in the art of resisting being practised upon.

New methods of education were filtering into the schools. No longer was it the duty of the teacher to hold the attention of the class. Now she had to cope with infant restlessness not by repression but by directing activity. The introduction of Broadcast lessons on the radio involved training pupils to listen which required preparation beforehand, concentration on the class and its responses at the time, and appropriate following up soon after.

The conclusion was that teaching practice had indeed widened as there was a far greater range of professional skills to be acquired. The student had to learn to be a thoughtful observer of children, a versatile yet reliable guide to many regions of experience, and a dispassionate and accurate recorder of experimental results.

The post-1930 students

Now that the Matriculation Certificate was the entrance requirement for all courses, students entering TC were a little older than previously. That brought with it a different set of problems. Sister Kate had already begun to tackle this in 1927 by the revision of rules and privileges. The College authorities aimed to give as much liberty as was in accord with the claims of training in order that the students would learn self-management. The age at which each division attained appropriate privileges was lowered, giving full seniority at the age of 20. The students' reaction to these changes may be gauged from an article printed in the College Magazine in the guise of a letter from the present students to the OGs. "First, we must tell you that in the South African History of the future there will be one epoch, *viz* the year 1927, which will stand out in golden letters studded in diamonds, perhaps too dazzling to the eyes of the OGs. This year marks a distinct change in the College life. So great is it that it has dared to take for itself the startling titles of "The College Reformation" or "The Emancipation of the College girl".

The new regime was carrying the revision of college rules a step further without removing what mattered most in the College. Ways of making the students feel more mature included the introduction of a more individual study method and giving students more say in college affairs. The College Log Book recorded two initial college meetings. The first was on 15 June 1931 when the staff and students met to discuss preparation rules. Each class was to try out its own scheme with mutual consideration and it was agreed to meet again to review decisions one month after the start of the next term.

The second meeting of the College took place on 10 July 1931. The agenda included discussion of the preparation arrangement arrived at, the College Song and Hymn, the suggestion about keeping Founder's Day each year on 14 November as the College birthday, and the possibility of a Choral Society. The Head Girl, a title harking back to the early days, was henceforth to be known as the Senior Student.

The matter of preparation was closely linked to that of self-discipline, but morning and evening preparation continued as previously and were compulsory. Each College class had the valuable experience of drawing up its own scheme for securing an atmosphere in which concentration was possible. The schemes were not very different from those originally propounded by the authorities but the responsibility for them had been shifted on to the students' shoulders. A sub-committee of class representatives dealt with inter-class questions such as the absolute silence of the Reference Library and the due regulation of legitimate conversation in the downstairs library. Preparation hours remained unchanged.

Sister Frances Mary felt that the prefect system was decidedly outdated for a training college and so the system was dropped. Sadly, many given freedom will misuse it. In 1938 the privilege of optional attendance at the daily morning and evening prayers in St Mary's given to third- and fourth-year students in 1931 was rescinded without any objections being raised. It had led to a good deal of merely casual non-attendance and gave the wrong impression of "privilege". Vigilance on the part of the staff was always necessary.

Iris Baisley (1931–32) recalled: "Sister FM decided to relax the rules on dress and behaviour and it went to the students' heads. Up to then they had been treated like school children… Sister FM decided to do away with regimentation and for two weeks there was bedlam."

The need arose to raise the matter of conduct generally. The Principal spoke of such matters as tidiness and the importance of assuming a measure of personal responsibility. Students were required to behave correctly at lectures and to be conscious of the need for punctuality. The students were reminded that the College was now on a post-matric basis and that this meant that more personal responsibility was needed. They should not still be at the stage of needing supervision.

College quarterly meetings

In 1931 College Quarterly Meetings of staff and students were instituted for the discussion of College policy. It was decided to abolish the navy-blue uniform and panama hat for first years but to keep the white dress for concerts. It was felt, and rightly so, that school uniform was no longer suitable for TC students. Further the name and office of "prefect" changed to that of "representative" and House Committees and a Students' Council were introduced with a carefully drafted Constitution designed to safeguard the stability of all good traditions and the central authority.

In the Magazine the College students wrote a letter to old students informing them that the first general College Meeting conducted solely by students had been held that term. The Senior Student, Alex Wood, officiated. This marked an epoch in the history of the College and would always be remembered by everyone present. The whole College attended and several subjects of interest to the students including the new prep system were fully discussed. The Principal reporting on this meeting commented that the students were beginning to handle their responsibilities better. The meetings provided the opportunity for the exchange of opinions.

The representatives were elected by the students and then later inducted. The Induction Service was conducted in the College Chapel and amounted to a corporate agreement. The representatives promised: "We, whom you have elected as your representatives, do here in the presence of God offer ourselves to serve you during this year as well as we are able, in truth and sincerity, without favour or partiality, for the good of this College and the greater glory of God." To which the Students replied: "We, who have elected you, do here, in the presence of God, accept you as our representatives, and promise you loyalty, confidence and true dealing, for the good of this College and the greater glory of God."

Jewish girls and Roman Catholics were admitted separately at College Meetings away from Chapel. Here we see an example of the open-mindedness and tolerance that characterised TC.

Reactions of the Sisters

Not all the Sisters were happy with the changes. The matter was raised at the Annual Chapter in January 1934. It was felt that in the life of the College there was the tendency towards more complexity in student life. Sister Dorothy felt that the students were becoming more extravagant. The reason given for this was that the students' home standard of living had risen implying a shift away from what Mother Cecile had intended. But things were changing! However much in the past it may have been the function of the College to train the impecunious and the immature to earn a decent livelihood, its function henceforth should increasingly be towards the training of leaders among their own generation and in their own country.

The fees at TC were £10 per quarter less than at Rhodes and were £10 more than at other training colleges. Sister Frances Mary said that the students were getting what they were paying for as the College was not out to make a profit. She pointed out that the fees at TC had to be higher than those at the Government colleges where students were boarded as well as taught for fees far below cost price. This was to be a recurring complaint at TC.

Widening the social circle – TC students and the airmen

In October 1941 the cat was really put among the pigeons where the House Sisters were concerned with the arrival in Grahamstown of the Royal Air Force (RAF). A new training camp had been opened for the training of pilots for the Air Force. At a meeting of the House Sisters on 17 October they discussed methods of entertaining the young men and how to co-operate with the authorities at the camp. The students were to be asked to join in devising plans for the entertainment of the young men. It was agreed to call a General College Meeting.

Were the Sisters over re-acting? Many thought so, but they were certainly taking their responsibilities *in loco parentis* most seriously. The Sisters might well have been heavenly-minded, but they were also worldly-wise. Since 1912 the Community had run St Monica's Home in Queenstown for those young white women who had fallen pregnant out of wedlock. This was something frowned on socially at the time. Some babies born in Queenstown were looked after at the Queen Alexandra Home for Babies in Grahamstown, and when they were older they were moved to the Woodville Orphanage. Both institutions were run by the Sisters. The House Sisters had reason to be worried.

At a College Meeting on 7 March 1942 it was agreed that all students who wished to go out with Air Force personnel had to have written permission from their parents. In no circumstances was a student to allow herself to be "picked up" when returning from Church or town. First year students with brothers in the Air Force were permitted to see them on Saturday afternoons and evenings and on Sundays. Then it was decided that it would be necessary for all students to have a letter sanctioning friendship with servicemen. The men were invited to dances at the College. These were held in the Beethoven Hall under the supervision of a Sister. An OG who trained during the war years and after the arrival of the RAF remembered clearly the lengthy list of new rules. She commented that the compensation was that they did not have to rely on Rhodes to supply partners for College dances.

The Second World War

The Second World War did not pass the College by entirely. Reminiscences help us to capture the situation at TC. As it was war time, Grahamstown was a hive of activity. Apart from the Army Camp, the RAF and SA Air Force had camps nearby. The latter were patrolling the coastline for German U-boats. College girls were not actively involved with the war but contributed to the war effort. They wrote to soldiers away from home to keep up their morale. They could join the Voluntary Aid Detachment

FAITHFUL TO THE VISION 61

(VAD)or Fire Fighting and were trained in First Aid and fire fighting in case Grahamstown was bombed. One OG (student 1943–1944) chose VAD and wore a special uniform. They had to assist at the Settlers' Hospital over the weekends and were given basic chores – emptying bedpans was the worst!

In case of bombing and the need to make a hurried exit, the students had to place their dressing gowns and slippers at the end of their beds each night. The gathering point was in Canterbury basement. There were black-out curtains so that no light showed. On Saturday evenings volunteers were collected by troop carriers and taken to the RAF/SAAF camps to dances. They were given light refreshments and obviously heavily chaperoned. At the end of the war special thanksgiving services were held throughout South Africa.

The ethos of the College and Religious Instruction

Sister Frances Mary wrote that, whatever tensions there were in the College or among staff and Sisters, there was always a background of prayer among the Sisters of which the students themselves were aware and in which they freely participated in their own attractive Chapel. Indeed, the whole working life was conducted against a background of petition with its complementary thanksgiving. This spiritual dimension was an integral part of life at TC and influenced the lives of all the students.

The Principal was always conscious of the aims of the College. The College was the property of a Religious Community founded primarily for the Glory of God and it was up to the Sisters to keep it true to this vision. Sister Frances Mary stated quite categorically that they did not wish to copy any other college. They wished to preserve the spirit in which the College had been founded and though it did not exist merely to carry out Departmental Regulations they endeavoured to show that Christianity made for a high standard of general efficiency.

The College authorities insisted on the observance of those aims for which the College existed: a commitment to Christian aims and ideals. The dilemma was that certain students felt they were unnecessary and could be ignored. In that case why had they chosen to train at TC? TC did more than prepare women for a teaching career; it set out to mould character and personality. In the College Magazine for May 1941 Sister Frances Mary had put this most forcibly: "The teacher is a worker in tissue of eternal value; she weaves the only fabric in the universe which has survival quality, for the soul alone is bomb-proof...in its essential personal being... Let us be sure of this: every moment of our work has this eternal significance as we recognise in each tiresome or helpful child the germ of a unique personality, it is not what the school will be next year, or whether it is working towards an A grade that matters – but what spirits it is fashioning day by day."

In 1934 changes were made in the arrangements for Scripture teaching in the College. Each student would in future be able to attend the class taken by her own minister. It was hoped that this arrangement would improve the pastoral influence of the clergy by providing opportunities for a better acquaintance between ministers and members of their flock which had not always been the case in the past. The Principal wrote that all the ministers had kindly agreed to give the new plan a trial and she hoped that it would add glory and value to the already wonderful work which they undertook in the College.

The Primary first and second year students were also taken once a week each for a longer period of instruction in the teaching of Scripture. They were divided into three groups – the DRC group taught by an Afrikaans speaking teacher; the English-speaking Free Church group taught by one of the residents of Winchester (a residence for staff members); and the Anglican group taught by a Sister. A continuous course of Old Testament teaching in the first year and New Testament in the second year was undertaken with the aim of providing the students with a thorough knowledge of the matter and method of the Scripture Ordinance to secure more systematic day and Sunday School teaching from them later.

After the outbreak of the Second World War, Sister Frances Mary writing in the College Magazine with the College students and OGs in mind entitled her article "Responsibilities of teachers: Propaganda or Not?" It raised some pertinent matters: She pointed out that current events had shown the power of an educational system to mould the habits and ideals of its citizens. She asked whether it was propaganda to put before children or adolescents the universal principles of all higher civilisation – ideals of mercy, truth, justice, temperance, brotherhood and service; and to allow them to sift the lessons of history and indeed of all the human arts and sciences by these standards. Was it propaganda to allow children of a professedly Christian country to study the documentary history of Christ's life?

Sister Frances Mary believed that spiritual training was not an infringement of the child's rights but that to which she had the deepest right. There should be no feeling of apology about meeting this need in the widest cultural and religious sense. For her no subject was of more significance than the ethical and spiritual education of youth. Even parents of assured religious belief often found it increasingly difficult to convey to growing children the spiritual groundwork of their own ethical standards.

New life and direction for Religious Instruction/Scripture Teaching

Religious Instruction in training institutions was governed by the Religious Instruction (RI) in Schools Ordinance No 18 of 1913 which was later incorporated in the Consolidated Education Ordinance (No 5 of 1921) where the emphasis was on the Catechism and a syllabus for Bible History. No special syllabus for training colleges was prescribed in this Ordinance nor was provision made in those institutions for RI as such. It was laid down that in all training institutions controlled by the Department the method of imparting religious instruction based upon the Catechism and the syllabus laid down in the Second Schedule to Ordinance No 5 of 1921 should be taught as an optional subject.

In July 1945 the Education Amendment Ordinance (No 10 of 1945) was promulgated. Its main feature was the new syllabus for religious instruction which Sister Frances Mary had played an important part in devising. It was more comprehensive than the former syllabus. It included all the standards and had been drawn up with great care and thoroughness. It provided an opportunity for rousing fresh interest among the students and hopefully for kindling a lasting zeal in many. It was hoped that it would give new life and direction to religious instruction in the schools of the Cape Province.

This led to an innovation at TC: the successful application of the group method to Scripture teaching. The new Scripture Syllabus was to be worked on self-activity lines involving the use of relevant books. The effect was magical. Scripture became a subject of foremost interest and students read widely outside the class periods as well and discussed religious topics from a totally new angle. No lectures were given but reference guides were supplied, and advice was available; each quarter the students also did some practical application work suitable for the classroom including art, handwork, speech and singing. They entered with zest into the experiment of more vital religious education in schools as did their practising schools with successful results.

TC and experimentation with teaching methods

The Principal and her staff felt that the educational authorities were inclined to cramp their activities. On the other hand, TC was a significant trail-blazer unashamedly used by the Department for experimentation. The Principal in a report to the English Helpers mentioned a Circuit Inspector present at the Founder's Day in 1939. The gist of his conversation with Sister Frances Mary was that private effort would always outrun official inertia. He felt it might well take five years for the Education Office to accept a change whereas TC appeared to include experimentation as a given. He referred to signs of change evident in schools where young teachers trained in Grahamstown were employed.

The Training College had achieved a unique place among the Training Colleges in South Africa. When asked by the Principal whether TC was free to continue experimenting with the curriculum and training in spite of the various official documents which were periodically served upon the training colleges, the SGE replied that TC should never be restricted by the Department, that their experimentation was welcomed and that they were trusted completely in this regard. This was indeed a remarkable commendation and reassurance.

Physical Training

From the earliest years physical activities had played an important part in the daily life of the students. In 1922 a Games Mistress was appointed for the first time. This was not a Departmental appointment; the salary had to be met from current funds. The routine work of training students to teach drill, games, eurhythmics and hygiene in the schools and of coaching their games meant that she had a full timetable.

By 1922 the College needed more land for sporting activities. This need had become acute with the increase in numbers, for by 1922 the roll numbered 275 students and more and more emphasis was being placed on physical education. Arrangements were made by the Department for another sports area. It was felt that adequate instruction in physical culture and games was important as an integral part of the life and activities of the training institution. It was also necessary in the day schools to which the students on completion of their studies would be attached. The SGE was sure that the new facility would prove a great acquisition to the institution which already occupied such a prominent position among the training institutions of the Province.

On 9 March 1936 the Manager wrote to the SGE concerning the employment of a Physical Training Instructress. She drew attention to the fact that Physical Training had become an integral part of the work of student teachers in training and that since the beginning of 1923 their management had provided a full-time instructress. She requested that this post be considered a Departmental one. Much of the work involved coaching students' games out of hours both for their own physical development and for their subsequent ability to take games in schools. A Departmental post was created later that year with the proviso that preference was to be given to a suitably qualified teacher holding the bilingual certificate. The Department agreed to recognise the post for the usual 2/3 salary grant.

Sister Frances Mary wrote to Miss Gerdener, an applicant for the post, that they had received Departmental sanction for her appointment to the newly created post in Physical Education at the College. Where sporting activities were concerned, students took part in tennis, hockey, netball, rounders or swimming; the enthusiastic few were engaged in all of them. An Old Girl remembered that they had to be able to coach and referee Netball, Hockey and Tennis. They had to play two hours of sport of their choice each week and record it in a book provided. Another OG remembered that College always seemed a rush – "onto Netball Court at 7.00 a.m. for gymnastics – winter and summer, followed by cold showers – rush to change – breakfast in the Hall – rush for Chapel – find a beret to wear – rush to lecture rooms. (Later) Principals always congratulated her on being TC trained."

Swimming

Swimming was gaining in popularity among the students. Up to that point the Graeme School swimming bath, over the road from the college in Somerset Street, had been hired on two days a week at a cost of £36 a year. The Principal felt this was not a satisfactory arrangement and so she spoke to the Community Chapter about the desirability of a swimming bath for the College. She was able to preface her request by saying that the Advisory Board was strongly in favour and besides most large schools and colleges had their own baths. The swimming bath was also required for the physical culture course which was then required by the Department and to keep up the standard of swimming. Sister Frances Mary pointed out that the estimated cost of bath with infiltration plant was approximately £2000. A little over £200 was in hand towards this cost. A loan of £670 free of interest had been offered and probably £1000 could be borrowed from the Diocesan Trustees and the interest covered by a Departmental grant-in-aid. Clearly the coffers were not over-flowing, and funding was a problem.

The site proposed was the area up the hill on Somerset Street behind Winchester where an open-air gymnasium was envisaged as part of the plan. The Principal had already approached Mr Carr a local contractor who would undertake the construction at a charge of 5% on outlay. The Sisters voted in favour of proceeding with the bath. The work of excavation took longer than expected but they were at the same time levelling up the site for the gymnasium. Concrete blocks were to be used in that construction as they were cheaper than brick. The latest estimated cost of the bath was £1350 and of the infiltration plant £1000. A loan of £1000 at 5% had been obtained from the Diocesan Trustees and an overdraft at the Bank up to £1500 at 5.5% would be allowed if it was necessary. This scratching around for finance was to be a regular part of each Principal's tenure of office. The swimming bath is still in existence today, but the gymnasium has long since disappeared.

Social Studies Circle

During the third quarter of 1936 a Social Studies Circle with an active Committee with student officers was formed in the College with the special object of studying such matters as world affairs, peace, and race-relationships. The members also showed a practical interest in what were then referred to as "Native Affairs". This led to the introduction of what became known in the College as "Bantu Students' Day". The visiting students from Healdtown, Lovedale and St Matthew's Training Colleges exchanged ideas with TC students, were shown handwork and classroom apparatus, and shared lunch together. The Principal wrote proudly, "While our own students picnicked outside (those who were not members of the Social Studies Circle), we were able to give our Bantu guests a meal in the Memorial Hall where – most wonderful of all – members of the Social Studies Circle and others sat at table, serving and eating with them. This and the general attitude of friendliness to fellow-students made a great impression on the visitors." These visits were reciprocated with TC students visiting the different Colleges. Owing to Government policy this interaction was subsequently discontinued.

Bilingualism

Hanging over the Principal's head all the time like the sword of Damocles was the matter of bilingualism. It was the major challenge of the time described as the "burning question" of the educational day. In 1938 yet another experiment was conducted in the College, namely an attempt at co-operative bilingualism which yielded exceptional results in the oral tests held by the Inspectors. This was intended to overcome the difficulty of securing actual oral practice in oral lessons.

The fruits of this endeavour were seen in the results when the English and Afrikaans oral work (i.e. reading and elocution) was submitted to the test. The general level of attainment was good, and the Inspector praised the work highly. They seemed to have turned a long and awkward corner in this regard. Some of the gain had come from the higher proportion of Afrikaans-speaking students and the increased tendency towards language interchange.

The Afrikaans-medium colleges had practically no English-speaking students whereas the few remaining English-medium colleges had quite a high and ever-increasing proportion of Afrikaans-speaking students. This combination of students from both European races had been one of the aims of the College from Mother Cecile's day as a means towards unity. The significant point was the decreasing number of English-speaking teachers being trained throughout the country.

An OG (1944–46) recalled: "How fortunate I was to have trained at TC – my parents' choice – having grown up in an Afrikaans town and speaking Afrikaans at home, I was thrown into the deep end at Lincoln but with a background of excellent English masters at school I was able to speak the language after a fortnight. In my 41 years of teaching all English schools were keen to have me on the staff because of my training at TC."

Efforts were constantly being made to improve the lower Afrikaans, for example by a continuous choral dialogue of everyday conversation which it was hoped would build up cumulatively throughout the year. This proved to be a popular way of doing it.

How was the staff of TC, set as they were in what had been described as a rather "narrowly and exclusively English country town", to carry out the requirement laid down for training colleges? The requirement stipulated that there should be a 50:50 division in the medium of instruction. In view of the strenuousness of the required training college courses it was a disheartening prospect. It would cause great staffing problems. Either the length of the teacher's course would have to be extended or the range or standard of the work to be covered would have to be reduced.

An OG recalling her arrival at College gives some idea of the range of subjects to be covered: "We started our teacher training on Monday 30 January and were in quite a shock as we had 22 different 'subjects' to learn. These included the methods of teaching the various sports, first aid, music, choirs, speech training, scripture, general method, art, library method, etc. Assignments in different subjects were done in groups in the beautiful library." However, the College was committed to a policy of dual-medium instruction within a period of five years, 1944–1949.

What seemed to be needed where this language dilemma was concerned was to break away from bookish knowledge of the language and instead to concentrate on a sound working knowledge of common speech forms. The Dramatic Society came to the rescue and One Act plays in both English and Afrikaans were frequently staged. The next principal would bring this to fruition.

Teaching students to think outside the box: Educational Principles

Grahamstown Training College offered a unique series of lectures entitled "Education Principles", the brain child of Sister Frances Mary. In the College Magazine of May 1936 is the statement: "Introduction of Educational Principles. The main object of these talks is an integrative, coordinating one, to direct attention to education so that we do not miss the wood for the trees." A CR Occasional Letter of 1946 described the "sideshows" happening at TC, among them being Educational Principles which it explained held a high place in the programme. Interesting and entertaining talks were given in the lecture theatre every Thursday afternoon by speakers with first-hand knowledge of the matter they were discussing.

The intention was that this series of talks with a wide human interest would broaden the outlook and enlarge the students' understanding of their fellow men and women. As was to be expected, the Principal was a frequent speaker. The talk on 13 February 1936 pointed to the bad points of the examination system and on the 20th covered the aims of education. The meeting on 27 February was on Bilingualism and the speakers were the Principal and Mr Theron. Miss Barrett spoke on the importance of Physical Education on 28 May.

Sister Frances Mary's notes of talks given by her at the Educational Principles meetings make truly fascinating reading. On 6 February 1936 she spoke about the teacher and primary education. The teachers in training were set high ideals. At TC it was a matter of less teaching and more learning. The spirit of absorption was what should be taken into the schools so that the children knew they were there to learn for the love of learning and not held there by the teacher either by personal magnetism or by physical force.

Later that month she spoke about the Aims of Education. The Principal mentioned that in the past the object was to give knowledge, "now it is to ensure what the child shall be". This required modifying the approach by answering the question: "What do we want the child to be?" The aim was to develop the individual: "We must try to come to his level, to put ourselves in his shoes." She felt that "teachers must be leaders and have some vision of what they are leading to", because "what you get in the child you get in the man, and thence in the nation... Working together with real interest and endeavour can be achieved if children never have inner resistances aroused. And this depends on the spirit of the teacher and of the home."

In 1950 a new curriculum for the Primary School was issued and was written up in the Education Gazette for November 1950. What this curriculum was introducing was what Sister Frances Mary had been talking about to the students at TC in 1936, and which that College had always seen as its objective in training of teachers. The new approach stressed not the subject matter but the new spirit which it was hoped would be aroused in the schools and so make a special contribution towards the development of desirable attitudes in the child; there was valuable knowledge that the child should acquire in the primary school as well as useful skills that she should learn.

The Introduction to the new course invited schools to consider the aim of primary education. "The mode of living of a society which has for its aim the happiness of all its members is based on the recognition and appreciation of the individual, as well as the individual's realisation of his obligation as a member of the community and his consciousness of his dependence on God." Hence the teacher was expected to create the right atmosphere in the school. She had to be able to put herself in the place of the child, character building and moral development being the goal.

Retirement of Sister Frances Mary

Sister Frances Mary retired in June 1946 and was granted leave of absence from the Community to pursue her studies. Later when it was apparent that she was not intending to return to the Community she was asked to leave. She became increasingly interested in furthering her studies in the paranormal. She wrote that throughout her life the subject of spiritual actuality had been a preoccupation.

OGs said that Sister Frances Mary had seldom made a rule without giving a reason, which had the desired effect of developing a sense of responsibility in her students and securing their co-operation. Her thirst for new ideas had many practical results. Her foresight contributed greatly to a change in Departmental policy regarding training colleges and their syllabuses. She had played a leading role in drawing up the syllabus for Religious Instruction in schools. Her influence had been felt throughout Southern Africa.

By all accounts Sister Frances Mary was a most remarkable woman with piercing dark blue eyes and a charisma of her own. Her presence was so overwhelming that the individual, however large the group, felt personally singled out and one's respect and admiration was the immediate response. Her leadership created a unique ambience which became a hallmark of the College. Sister Margery called Sister Frances Mary "a slave-driver": it had to be done if Sister Frances Mary decreed so! An OG mentioned that Sister Frances Mary had written the textbook they used so the students always had the uncomfortable feeling that she was psycho-analysing them.

Sister Frances Mary held an honoured place in the world of education. She was a recognised authority on Psychology not only in South Africa but also in Britain and her book, *Conduct and Ability*, dealing with this subject gained attention in authoritative circles as a work of originality and valuable thought. Subsequently as Miss Frances Banks she returned to England where she began lecturing on world religions. Her work took her to women's prisons and then to those of men, who petitioned for a further course. She became involved in the work of rehabilitation for those leaving prison and needing help in a world of action after years inside.

Alan Paton wrote that she was a woman of tremendous force of character and tremendous will-power. He described this as an eagle-like quality in her. An Inspectress recorded that often when she met a devoted and dedicated teacher she discovered that she had done her training under Fanny. She had been told again and again how decisive and permanent Frances Mary's inspiration was.

She was remembered thus by two OGs: "Sister Frances Mary had a gift which distinguished her – it was the gift of a compelling, infectious enthusiasm" (Enid Mills). "Sister Frances Mary, Frances Banks, was a lady ahead of her time...she was a natural leader, inspirational and radiating joy. As an educationalist she brought new freedoms (and got rid of the black stockings!) but she set high standards and did not suffer fools gladly. Many ideas now associated with New Age Philosophy were aired in class discussions during her 25 years with the CR" (Margaret Baines, later Lady Tredgold).

Extensions to Campus under Sister Frances Mary
The Library

In 1931 it was decided to convert the Assembly Room (a large class-room) into a library. Shelves were put up and oak tables and chairs were ordered from the Oxford Furnishing Company at a cost of £105.5.00. The Magazine elaborated on this: There were eight polished tables and 50 comfortable high-backed chairs. There were large convenient book cases standing out into the room to hold the books most of which were accessible to students for the first time. It was well used. It was felt that it would play a large part in teaching the students the pleasure and value of intensive study. Next required was a round table for the periodicals and better lighting. Electricity had come to the College in 1924. Before that gas was used.

In 1933 the library was extended through the needlework room by the removal of the folding doors. Four extra tables were added plus glass-fronted bookshelves for books which could not be removed from the library. There were now 25 sets of open bookshelves which were rapidly filling up. There were also certain subject libraries for example in the School of Music. The fiction library was housed in a room on another floor. The extended library was a handsome well-lit room where it was possible to seat the whole college comfortably and provide a pleasing setting for occasional lectures.

The Department of Education was anxious to encourage training colleges to develop libraries by offering annual library grants. In November 1935 the Magazine noted that many new books had been added to the library as the Education Department had given a three-quarter grant so that by spending £16 the College could get £64 worth of books. These departmental grants proved of the greatest value to TC. "Last year (1936) the Department contributed three quarters of £92 worth of books, and this year (1937) it is contributing the same proportion towards £120 worth of books at special contract prices. This has enabled us not only to extend our range, but also to buy a number of copies of the most-used reference books." When the College closed in 1975 all these books had to be packed up and sent off to the new training college in Port Elizabeth! The library was outgrowing its space and a new building was clearly needed.

The College had always stressed the importance of reading and the library was a well-used area. The entrance requirement for students had been raised to matriculation standard so the Principal and her staff were anxious to increase the range of the students' reading and the depth and maturity of their work. This would be achieved by giving the students free access to the excellent reference and other books which of necessity were stored either in the Staff Room or in locked cupboards. When the Assignment Method was introduced access to a good reference library became imperative.

It was apparent to the authorities at TC that a new library was urgently required. The pressing need though was finance. Initially the College was able to raise funds by appealing to friends in England, but this had not happened since the completion of the Memorial Hall. With the passage of time it became apparent that the money required for development ought to be raised in the country itself and not abroad. It was felt that the College having proved its use to South African citizens, should call upon their support to increase its effectiveness in line with modern requirements. The alternative was to seek a loan.

Discussions concerning the new building got under way in 1936. At a Council of Finance Meeting on 21 August the Superior drew attention to the dilapidated state of the building known as The Grotto. This property had been bought in 1902 by Mother Cecile and the main teaching block had been built on part of it in 1904. What remained was an old house wedged between the main teaching block and the Memorial Hall on the Grey Street frontage. In 1933 the lower floor of The Grotto had been turned into a tea room for students.

The discussions centred on whether to spend money on The Grotto or to demolish it and go ahead and build. If they chose the latter course, there were two options: either a building just for educational purposes or one combining educational with boarding facilities. A building solely for educational purposes was decided upon. Once again, the question of money for building was raised because £6500 was still owing to the Community on Beethoven House and money would have to be borrowed for further building.

The matter was raised again in August 1938. This time the Mother brought plans which Mr Kendall had sent for the proposed building on The Grotto site. The cost was estimated at about £12 000. Of this £3000 was in hand. Methods were then discussed for obtaining the money and after much thought and deliberation it was unanimously agreed to ask Mr Kendall to proceed with the plans so that the work might begin in December 1938.

By July 1939 after many negotiations a loan of £3000 from the Diocesan Board had been arranged at 5% p.a. The Community lent £1600 and promised another £400. Sir Thomas Graham had laid the Foundation Stone of the new building on 22 April 1939. On that occasion he appealed to those present to help the College secure contributions with which to meet the necessary outlay on the new building. This was the first time any direct appeal had been made to the citizens of Grahamstown for funds for the College and Sir Thomas hoped there would be a good response. He said there was a dire need for the new building for with the rapid development of the College and the methods of teaching used in the College it was necessary to have more accommodation for the library. Practically the whole first floor of the new building would be taken up by the library. The building was opened on Founder's Day 1939.

The guest speaker on Founder's Day was Inspector Hobson who also officially opened the new building. He mentioned the unique contribution which TC was making in education and stressed the sacrifice and widespread generosity which had made the new building possible. He referred to the new conditions which had made it necessary, especially the more individual ways of working which he considered among the greatest contributions which TC was rendering the country in the service of education. He said that already through the experimental efforts of the College he found evidence in his circuit of more individual methods of working and he hoped the College would persevere in its attempts to replace the lecture method by the activity of the pupil.

Mary Travers-Jackson [Jourdan] writing in the TC Magazine as a member of the Library Committee was clearly thrilled with the new reference library referred to by the students as "The Ref". "The building fund was born...and now in its stead stands a building, resplendent in its youth and brightness, inculcating its ideals – 'where wisdom entereth the Lord will bless'– into all that frequent it. The new 'Ref' is roughly in the shape of an H; in the middle stands the librarian's office and the stairs leading to the third floor... On either side of the main aisles are alcoves formed by the various subject shelves, and in these alcoves are placed three chairs and tables from the old 'Ref'; students are able to sit next to the subject shelf with which they are working on any night as the seating capacity of the 'Ref' is 130. This seating arrangement abolishes unnecessary noise and movement."

Music School

In 1935 the Music School was invited by the Education Department to give a course of weekly educational broadcasts in the fourth term of that year. Mr Archie Iliffe-Higgo wrote a series of short lectures on "The Ages of Music". Musical illustrations would be given by soloists or by a small orchestra and choir. TC was highly honoured in being chosen. Once again TC had been called upon to do pioneer work as this was the first occasion on which any School of Music had provided a complete series of educational broadcasts. These broadcasts were transmitted from the Grahamstown Broadcasting Station.

Grahamstown Training College had also had the privilege of contributing the major portion of the programme at the opening of the broadcasting studio in June 1935. That occasion had been recorded in the Log Book: "On 6 June the first evening programme broadcast from the Grahamstown studio: all 15 items in two-hour programme provided by TC students and staff. The programme included the *Brandenburg* concerto in B flat by the TC Orchestra." There were similar occasions in subsequent years when TC soloists and the orchestra were invited to broadcast a programme of music.

Towards the latter part of the 1930s reviews of concerts in *Grocott's Mail* point to the thoroughness of the training being given in the Music School. The College Orchestra was noted as being in particularly good form. In 1938 regular attendees at concerts had become accustomed to hearing music of a high standard, well prepared and presented by students. In many cases these students not only distinguished themselves in these concerts but continued to do well in other parts of South Africa and overseas. There was no doubt that that branch of the work of TC was an important contribution to the musical education of the province.

Following a concert on 8 November 1942 *Grocott's Mail* drew attention to the good audiences that always attended the concerts offered by the Music School and suggested that this was testimony to the enjoyment which was received from them and to the fact that music could still be one of the principle forms of solace in those stressful times.

In 1940 Mr Iliffe-Higgo suggested including more on the dramatic side in the concerts. This brought with it its own difficulties as there was no stage in the hall merely a raised section at one end. It was just possible to stage a play there but moving the seating required for the musical part of the programme would be inconvenient.

It was also suggested by the music staff that the formality of the musical evenings should be abandoned and that the students should be allowed to dress as they pleased not necessarily in white. Clearly the approach in the Music School was more relaxed than in the College itself. In February 1946 the Principal reminded the music staff of the College custom of addressing students as "Miss". Some discussion took place and it was conceded that Christian names might be used for small groups and individual lessons but that surnames should be used for choirs, large classes and the orchestra.

Examination results continued to bring honour to the Music School and its staff. In the examinations in 1943 for the Piano Licentiate Diploma which were conducted by examiners appointed by UNISA, two pupils of Mr Iliffe-Higgo achieved the unusual distinction of obtaining the double diploma of Performer and Teacher. This was a record for Grahamstown and probably for South Africa.

In the University Examinations in 1945 the Music School enjoyed exceptionally good results. In the final grade no fewer than eleven students were successful (100%) with five honours and two honourable mentions. In Piano Teacher's Licentiate two students were distinguished as the two best teachers in the Union and Southern Rhodesia.

On the surface all seemed well. The public continued to enjoy the concerts, but underneath cracks were appearing. Miss Margaret Dewar an OG and a member of the orchestra wrote to Sister Frances Mary in July 1942 that she had felt for a long time that if the students themselves were not interested in the orchestra as a College activity its essential purpose had been lost. One wanted to see youth there, not a handful of elderly people on the platform at concerts. Mr James MacLachlan joined the staff in 1934 and remained until 1942. Sister Frances Mary had written to him before his appointment warning him that the post had fallen in value and in the number of hours the College could guarantee. She ascribed this to the depression and the increase of mechanical music.

There were also the many changes which were evident in the 1930s. Those years saw increasing use of motor cars, the advent of "Talkies", the spread of the wireless, and all the outside attractions which led to a certain passivity and individualism in the choice of amusements. The result was a decrease in communal intra-college interests and in the personal efforts and loyalties which arose from them. Sister Marjorie, who had been associated with the School of Music and the College since 1917, writing in 1969 expressed the opinion that College was more "homey" in the past when they had their own internal entertainments and fun compared with the present time when the students looked beyond the institution for their entertainment.

CHAPTER 6

TC under Sister Truda
1947–1957 and 1961–1962

SISTER TRUDA HAD had a distinguished academic career at Rhodes and Oxford Universities complemented by an equally outstanding sporting record as a hockey player, including representing the Eastern Cape. She was also an Oxford Blue. At Rhodes University she lectured in Zoology and was Head of Department from 1933 to 1935. She then registered at TC as a student and completed the Primary Teacher's Certificate. She joined the Community of the Resurrection of Our Lord during that time. She had a wide experience and understood students. Under her guidance the College continued along the lines already laid down by previous Principals; it was more than living up to its reputation. Students were expected to give of their best. Numbers in the KG course for instance were seriously down and the reason given for this was the reputation of their Infant School course for overworking its students. Consequently, several changes were introduced which it was hoped would achieve the same standard of training with less arduous and time-consuming effort.

It was still the unswerving purpose of the College to prepare well-trained teachers with a solid Christian background for the schools of the country.

Staffing problems

Sister Truda was extremely dissatisfied with the work ethic of the students. She made it clear at a College meeting that the students were not engaged on a university course where it was possible to cram for the examinations. They were undergoing a professional training for a specific professional career. Their results would be judged by their whole two years' performance which was the system employed at TC at that time. The staff had to be able to satisfy themselves that the work had been done. There was no place for the lazy student or a last-minute panic with this system. Attendance at lectures was not an optional extra.

This inevitably placed a tremendous burden on the staff, as the Inspectors pointed out. The hours of work expected of the staff were not seen as unduly onerous, but the Inspectors agreed that the methods used at TC together with the preparation and correction of assignment work made big demands; more so than in colleges where the method of straight lecturing and end-of-year final exams was still employed.

The Inspectors acknowledged that the staff went more than the extra mile in that they did a considerable amount of individual coaching and supervision of students' teaching practice which received strong emphasis in the training course at this College. TC was extremely fortunate in the members of its staff who were described as highly trained and conspicuous for their loyalty and devotion to the College. At this period the staff comprised fourteen lay members and three teaching Sisters all of whom were employed on an equal footing by the Cape Education Department. The proportion of lay staff and teaching Sisters was clearly unbalanced. The kind of service given when there were more teaching Sisters was no longer available.

As early as 1939 the Superior had spoken of the shortage of teaching Sisters in the Community. This problem was to be exacerbated as the years passed. The Community was not attracting new members to its ranks and by 1959 the number of old Sisters dying exceeded the number of Sisters being professed into the Community.

Above all the College was in financial difficulties. It was feeling the financial stringency of increased cost-of-living, increased salaries, and the decreased income from the smaller enrolment of students, which was a feature of the post-war years. Undoubtedly one way of correcting that situation would be to have more teaching Sisters on the staff, for it was their salaries which had earlier been used for College purposes especially when lay staff salary increases were required.

The post-war shortage of teachers in the Cape Colony was acute and affected TC. Furthermore, there had been far too many staff changes at the

College for the efficient and smooth working of the courses. The smooth running of the College had also suffered a great deal from staff sick-leave. The positive factor was that past students were always welcomed back on to the staff. In 1951 there were seven OGs on the staff.

Sister Truda was clearly an outspoken person. Her frustration over the staffing situation is seen in her correspondence over the years. She wrote to Miss Gerdener at the Mowbray Training College, "...I was very disappointed to find that she (Miss Hughes), was wanting to leave us so soon, but these young people seem to get restless in small centres... There is no such word as 'obligation' in their vocabulary!" The College had moved from a comfortable staffing position in the early 1940s to a critical situation by the late 1950s as fewer applications were received from candidates willing and able to make a long-term commitment. In March 1966 the Principal, by then Sister Virginia, wrote to the Secretary of the Examinations Branch of the Education Department that students taking Afrikaans Higher in their second year in 1965 had been handicapped in their work in this subject. The previous year the lecturer in Afrikaans Higher was not a satisfactory teacher. In fact for the first quarte of 1965 Afrikaans Higher had been in the hands of a temporary non-graduate lecturer until the arrival in April of Mr van der Mescht. Here the spotlight was thrown on the problem of getting good teachers of Afrikaans in Grahamstown.

Staffing problems continued. Part of the difficulty lay in retaining young members of staff. They were happy in their work in the College but admitted to being terribly lonely in Grahamstown. From 1960 for all permanent appointments at training institutions a higher grade Bilingual Certificate (AE) would be required. At that stage Agriculture, Art, Domestic Science, Handwork, Music and Physical Education were exempted from this condition. This requirement only added to the burdens of finding suitable staff.

The Department had already acknowledged the problem of finding graduate teachers. In 1954 permission was given for teachers from abroad to be imported providing the vacant post had been advertised in two successive issues of the Education Gazette without any response from suitable South African applicants. Teachers from overseas were required to undertake to qualify bilingually within a period of three years. What this concession did not make clear was the immense amount of red tape that had to be surmounted prior to permission being given, a provision that became more and more difficult to achieve as the years passed. The South African Government required a great deal of information including references, medical examinations and X-rays, as well as an affidavit from the Principal that the applicant was to be employed at TC. Once all this had been submitted to Pretoria it took more than three months for a permit to be issued.

At the end of 1957 the Superior's unexpected decision to send Sister Truda to Mapanza in Zambia, with the intention of appointing Sister Madeline as the next Principal met with resistance from the Department. The Department was not prepared to approve of the permanent appointment of a non-graduate to the principalship of the Training College. The temporary appointment of Sister Madeline as Principal was approved of from 1 April 1958 to 31 December 1958. The post would have to be advertised as from 1 January 1959. The chief Inspector was told that Sister Madeline was acceptable to both staff and students. He replied that there was nothing whatsoever against the permanent appointment, except the lack of a degree. In the event, Sister Madeline's term of office was extended beyond the agreed date until Sister Truda was recalled from Mapanza.

Sister Truda was brought back from Mapanza and resumed the principalship of the College for a further period. The Superior wrote to the Chief Inspector that there were many changes imminent as older tried members of staff were now reaching retirement age. For that reason, she considered it essential that Sister Truda should continue to head up the College. She reported that Sister Virginia had made a good start on the staff and was fitting in happily. Sister Truda's appointment was extended into 1961 and this gave the College a sense of stability. Her tenure was then extended to enable her to hand over the reins to Sister Virginia during 1962. After her retirement Sister Truda returned to Mapanza and was later moved to St Andrew's House in Bulawayo.

The Superior also mentioned the matter of Sister Ada Raphael who did not hold a science degree, but she said it would be difficult to find a science graduate steeped in high school teaching who would be interested in Nature Study in the tradition which Sister Irene established at TC. The bottom line was that they were not usually inundated with applications for their posts as people were rather shy of undertaking training college work.

The nature of the staff may be judged by the length of service many of them gave to TC. They were maiden ladies of the old school type. They gave of their all to the College and are remembered by many OGs with affection. The College was also well served by many Sisters both on the teaching staff and in the Hostels. Long after the Community found it impossible to supply teaching Sisters for the College staff, Sisters were still responsible for the Hostels where many had a lasting influence on the students who in their relations with the Sisters soon came to see the "human in the habit"!

The Community

From its inception the Community had been largely but not entirely a teaching Order. In its early years the Community grew rapidly and as a result undertook more and more work. By the late 1920s the Community was involved in many works both in South Africa and beyond the border. During the 1930s the Community began to find that it could not supply Sisters to staff all the work that had been undertaken. There was an urgent need for young teaching Sisters. By the end of the 1940s the Community had begun withdrawing from work they had established.

In the years between 1940 and 1970, 61 women were professed into the Community and 77 members died. There were no further professions before 1975.

By 1963 there were only about 50 active Sisters. There were eleven Branch Houses as well as the work in Grahamstown (which included other undertakings apart from TC). The situation thereafter merely worsened and there were fewer and fewer Sisters available for the staff of TC.

Anne Semple who was at TC from 1973–1975 recalls that they had only one Community Sister during their three years and that was Sister Joyce Mary who taught Maths. There were Miss Clayton and Miss Atkinson (Helpers from England) – the students didn't really know whether they were nuns or not. But the students generally had little to do with the Community of the Resurrection and only saw the Mother Superior once or twice a year.

Students vs College Rules

Before her departure, Sister Frances Mary had had the College Rules completely revised. During 1946 and 1947 Sister Truda and Edith Judge, Senior Student 1947, had a difficult time over the House rules which had not been revised. Meetings were held and the dozens of rules re-written.

Concerning these troubles Sister Truda wrote a personal letter on 15 December 1986 to Mrs Edith Blackbeard (as Edith Judge she had been Senior Anglican Student 1946 and then Senior Student in 1947): "I was always very conscious of being in succession to a very great Principal (Sister Frances Mary), but she and I both felt that God had brought me there to build and consolidate on her foundations."

In a lengthy postscript to the same letter Sister Truda wrote: "When Frances Mary was preparing me for the handover, she said she had concentrated her efforts on the Academic side of the College.

"She had not been able to update Hostel life. She expected me with my university background to do that. She said ominously, 'When a Principal retires after a long time, overdue changes are bound to push to the surface. I expect you to meet an explosion in the Hostel life.' And explosion we did have!!!

"My policy was, 'Well, let them work it out for themselves. If they don't like petty rules, let's make a clean sweep and do without any Rules until they find out what they want.' I thought that was exactly what we did. You came back to me to say the students were sick of each other and their lack of consideration for each other, and they wanted Rules. So I invited the Student Council and Heads of Houses to formulate the rules they needed... I was well satisfied that the plan had worked. The Students discovered for themselves they needed rules; the Student Council formulated what they felt were needed, and I ratified them."

The Sisters wanted to give the students the freedom they had asked for provided they could develop in the students a sense of inward self-restraint and responsibility. The wisdom of Solomon was clearly a prerequisite where the handling of the students was concerned.

A group of the students had attended a National Union of South African Students (NUSAS) Conference at the University of the Witwatersrand in the winter holidays in 1951 and had returned to the College filled with great ideas. Sister Truda described how the students wanted to be better informed and better educated. They were quite ready with ideas as to how best to improve the rest of the College. At a College Meeting they set out their requests in "moderate and well-balanced" terms: they desired greater freedom and responsibility. At the same time, they were ready to accept the need for sacrifice if they were to maintain a high standard of work in a heavy course of professional training based on a system of internal examination.

It was obvious that week-nights were time for study; this was non-negotiable. But by the same token they felt that the time had come for them to assume greater responsibility and to decide for themselves when they were able to have a night off. An OG recalled that in the 1950s they had plenty of rules and some students found them tiresome and too much like the boarding schools from which they had so recently been set free. There was so much work that they didn't really have a lot of time for gallivanting.

The student leaders were sure that a good proportion of the students would not abuse such freedom and that few if any would in fact make use of the concession every week; it was just the feeling that they were free to do so if they wished that was important. A suggestion was put that the staff should be free to withdraw such a leave concession in cases where work or health seemed to suffer.

The recollections of OGs would suggest that most of those at the College felt that they were receiving something special and they therefore took advantage of the opportunity. Wendy van Schalkwyk (Scott) 1963–1965 admits "as I grow older I realise what a profound effect TC had on me." Helen Fenwick (Pneumaticos) 1971–1973 felt "how privileged we had been to attend TC." And Margot van Niekerk (Vosloo) 1963–1964 thinks back "with fond memories to my two years at TC. The foundations laid by the staff are precious."

Just how were the authorities to reach and maintain a compromise acceptable to the students or at least the outspoken ones? Attendance at Chapel was raised many times, but it is interesting to note that one of the special memories retained by OGs was just that. "For all our antics and so-good-for-the-soul 'silliness' during our years in the 60s, strangely enough we never ever thought of bunking Chapel. Somehow it sort of held us together at the end of each day – it really was a very special, quiet time that we all seemed to appreciate. And miraculously, that attitude still prevails. (Whenever we are in Grahamstown for Reunions) we head straight for 'our' beautiful College Chapel. It was the heart of TC way back then, and remains so for us, even now."

It was felt that the old rules were too detailed and meticulous and outmoded. The students wanted to be more on a university basis. The chaperonage rules were greatly relaxed. Chaperonage was becoming an increasingly difficult matter and TC had always had strict rules in this regard. Now students were permitted to go for walks with men friends provided that first and second year students went out in parties. During the Sunday afternoon visiting hour they were permitted to go out alone.

The Principal and staff hoped that increased trust would in turn create greater personal responsibility and a determination to uphold the tone of the College. It had been pointed out to the students that rules were not intended to be a restriction of freedom. They were for the guidance of the students and for the convenience of all in the College. The revisions had been preceded by a great deal of thought and discussion and prayer. They were intended to ease the problems of corporate living. They were put to the College Meeting on 8 December 1947 and carried.

Acknowledging that TC may have been rather "rule encased", more so than other post-school institutions, the Principal felt that the students nevertheless did accept them as reasonable and necessary; provided the House Sisters exercised them on a basis of expecting courtesy and consideration they usually met with a fair measure of goodwill. The rules were intended to be a framework for training the students to be disciplined, considerate, and reliable members of a school staff.

Necessary changes

The College authorities were coming to the realisation that post-war students were different and that in their demands they were not slow to take advantage of the change in principalship with the retirement of Sister Frances Mary and the advent of Sister Truda. The students requested several far-reaching changes. They wanted the evening meal at 6.30 p.m. instead of 6.00 p.m. Following on this it was agreed that the Houses would be kept open all evening allowing students wanting to go to bed early access to their cubicles. It was also agreed that Common Rooms would be available for students who felt that rest or re-creative handwork or reading was legitimate for that evening. In this way it was hoped to ensure the continuance of the work atmosphere of the College block.

These changes were inevitably to result in structural alterations within the Houses where the students slept in cubicles but with dormitory-style lighting which meant a lights-out time each evening. The College Hostels were originally built for students who had completed an Elementary or Primary Education and who were satisfied with a boarding school regime and dormitory accommodation. The Matriculated students post-1931 had with good humour adjusted themselves to TC tradition which meant sleeping in cubicles and obeying the lights-out bell necessitated by the dormitory lighting.

The time had obviously come for the authorities to weigh up carefully what was of permanent value and what belonged to a period of the College's history now long past its usefulness. In a Quarterly Report the Principal mentioned, for instance, the veto against visiting cafés on a Sunday and a provision that dancing on a Saturday night must end in time for students to be in bed before midnight. She felt that students found it difficult to distinguish between essentials and non-essentials.

The students coming to the College were girls of their time. By 1957 there appeared to be a prevailing opinion that the students were a noisy, impossible and undisciplined crowd. The Principal attributed that to the general problems encountered in the schools from which they came. What was of concern to the staff were the reports of noisy and rude behaviour outside College precincts. "Our reputation has always stood high in town but is suffering some eclipse at present. The general political stress and tension is affecting the College, but we are trying hard to keep a spirit of unity and goodwill in the midst of opposing viewpoints."

In all this reorganisation and change there were certain things that were not negotiable and the chief of these concerned religious observance and practice. An early letter of Mother Cecile quoted in the College Magazine puts this succinctly: "You know my own view has never varied; the work has always seemed to me immensely valuable from a religious point of view, not ignoring the pleasure of sending, I trust, some teachers out into their life's work to clear and not confuse the brains of the children entrusted to them."

The College was a Church and Community foundation and therefore it was not possible to remove entirely from the rules the statement that all students were expected to attend their own place of worship on Sundays. The College authorities had taken upon themselves from the outset the responsibility for the students' spiritual well-being as part of the all-round development of body, mind and spirit which was the aim stressed by the Founder.

The Principal did concede that a custom which had grown up of "harrying defaulters" was to be discontinued. She had in mind the concept of personal responsibility and the need to exercise an example and influence which would inspire thinking students to undertake voluntarily the obligation of Church life. An OG Margaret Lloyd commenting on this aspect of College life noted "It has always amazed me how deeply we were influenced and nurtured spiritually in this special place. In just three years we were blessed so deeply it affected our lives from then on."

Among the non-negotiables was the fact that TC had a relatively small student body of about 200 students which the College authorities had no intention of enlarging. With that number it was possible to keep a close and personal relationship with each student and so avoid the impersonal character of a large university. There were some students who slipped through the net as the following story suggests. Ethne Fincham was at TC 1941–1943. She records her experience: "When I enrolled at College in 1941 after my parents had moved from the Kuruman district in the Northern Cape to settle in Grahamstown, I was completely overawed by my new surroundings. The beautiful city, the tarred streets, the huge, elegant College buildings, and the 'hundreds' of young ladies, were all a challenging experience for me. As a 'day-pot' I felt very 'out' of it all, and although I was affiliated to Lincoln House, I only went there once, and then only as far as the verandah... I used to study and use the Reference Library from about 5 to 7 in the evenings to give me access to the books while the students were in their respective houses before dinner and during dinner time. I used to walk home in the dark along dimly lit Huntly Street, passing the Good Shepherd School on my way, clutching my locker key firmly in my fist for protection! It was war time and the streets were deserted, so I need not have been afraid... I am grateful for my College days and cherish the opportunity I had to grow in so many ways and to emerge eventually as a fully-fledged teacher."

By 1951 the Principal reported that she felt the students were learning to appreciate the fact that corporate worship among confirmed members of Christian denominations in a Christian institution in a Christian country was an obligation independent of their passing moods and feelings. She mentioned that the prayers of the Sisters for the students in the last few weeks of their College course were centred on the personal aspect of their spiritual development, the deepening of their prayer life, and their personal Christian commitment.

Change was in the air, but it was difficult to discern just how much all these changes especially the leave facilities were affecting the work done by the students. The staff was anxious about the standard of the work handed in: "so much of it is merely done, just to get it handed in and out of the way and is superficial and unthinking." There was also an attitude of taking more and more and being unwilling to accept a NO to any request.

Later the Principal felt that the work seemed mediocre and that there was no great zest for learning. It seemed that there were too many distractions to allow for a scholarly attitude towards work. She admitted that most students were alert, sensible and capable along practical lines and made good primary teachers.

The Training College had always prided itself on the fact that it gave students attending the College a true professional training. Sister Truda referred to this again and again. She stressed that teachers bore a "stamp" or a "mark". "A great deal is expected of teachers – not only that they should be competent and conscientious, but that they should have high standards of personal integrity. You are marked women in the community which expects you to live up to those high standards. When you teach, the children will watch you and take their tone and their lead from you."

Those who were trained at TC left with a distinct mark upon them and over the years of its existence people had come to expect certain standards from those bearing that particular mark because as a College "we expect, and try to inculcate, high standards of work and professional responsibility. But more than that – we expect and aim for high standards of personal conduct. Why else do you suppose that we lay such emphasis on personal integrity, basic honesty, behaviour, deportment and uprightness?"

Speaking to first-year students at the start of 1958 Sister Truda put this another way: "As teachers you must accept the fact that you must always watch deportment, behaviour, dress... Parents and critics will watch and criticise any slips. You are a model for children. We expect decent, modest, seemly behaviour. Remember you will be known everywhere as TC girls: outsiders judge the College by your conduct and behaviour. The tone and reputation of the College is in the hands of the student body." Yet the Principal exclaimed incredulously: "Principals of schools are falling over themselves to appoint our inexperienced students."

The Principal and the Student Council: To change or not to change?

With the Students' Representative Council (SRC), a Senior Student, general College Meetings, House Committees, Hostel Sisters' Meetings and Staff Meetings, the Principal now had a good communications network in the College. It was the responsibility of the Student Council to maintain the good tone of the College. The members were in close touch with the general life of the College and with the thought and conduct of the students. It was possible for them to correct any undesirable trends even before they became apparent to the staff. The Principal stressed the individual responsibility of each councillor but if the council member encountered difficulties she could not handle herself she should consult the Senior Student. Any matters of which the councillors disapproved were to be reported to the Principal immediately. The Student Council had no statutory powers, but it was encouraged to offer recommendations to the Principal.

The Student Council proved itself to be of value as the members were willing to give a lead in such issues as greater self-discipline and general orderliness. Sister Truda met with this body once a quarter to provide the SRC with guidance and to allow it to communicate student feelings and requests. She soon realised that the SRC had more standing with the students when they could see what it was achieving. There was a good deal of give and take but the SRC did help in maintaining discipline and tone.

The Reports given by the Senior Student show what the aims of the SRC were for their year of office. For instance in 1956 the SRC set itself three main aims: to increase the feeling of unity in the College with more interaction between staff and students; to encourage self-discipline by a more conscientious observance of quiet times and silent zones (e.g. the library); and to make the students as happy as possible during their time at College by ensuring that the door bell was always answered and that matters were communicated to College promptly.

The year following the SRC set itself the objective of maintaining the good tone and discipline of the College by furthering and building on the aims of the previous SRC and working for better facilities for students' visitors. The Senior Student mentioned that what had been achieved were loyalty and happiness; self-discipline had still not been realised!

The SRC of 1957 endeavoured to introduce several innovations intended to foster team spirit. In future all sports results were to be announced to the whole College. That year TC took part in Rhodes Rag. There was a Christmas Dinner attended by both staff and students. A request was made for a Current Events Board detailing current affairs. Students were encouraged to collect stamps for the Braille Library. Afrikaans hymn books were purchased for Lecture Theatre Prayers and on Fridays students were to speak Afrikaans at meals.

In May 1959 the Rhodes Rag Committee again invited TC to participate in the Rag procession on the Saturday morning. Careful thought was given to the matter. The Principal was concerned that too much time would be spent on the preparation of the Rag float, time which ought to be spent in pursuit of the professional study needs of the students. TC students were reminded that university students had more time available during the day than students pursuing a professional course. Preparations should in no way interfere with college work. The students were given strict instructions that those working on the float were to be correctly dressed: they had to be dressed from neck to knee as at Rhodes.

The Rhodes students were obviously keen to cultivate relations with TC. Rhodes men were much in demand as dance partners as an OG fondly remembered: "What scheming went on to get partners for dances. If one girl in your group knew a student at Rhodes, the poor fellow would be asked to get the required number of blind dates for your friends. Once he had them, there was the matching up of tall and short – all by telephone. You hadn't a clue, when you were called to the hostel door, who you were going to find, and most of your friends who were still waiting for their dates were hanging out the windows to see who you had got. Some were fine, and some were disasters."

TC students and Rhodes University activities

The Training College students were not denied the fun of joining in with Rhodes on occasion. OGs recalling their time at TC in the 1960s mentioned that TC students joined in many Rhodes activities. Most notably this included the annual Rhodes Rag. They were given large bundles of magazines to sell and took part in float building and of course Rag. Many a TC girl was gated for returning from float-building evenings beyond curfew hour. There were also serious moments. The 1960s were difficult times politically as resistance to the oppression of the apartheid regime increased. There were student protests around the country. Sit-ins were held – usually outside the Rhodes Great Hall – in which TC students participated to demonstrate their solidarity with Rhodes students. They were part of a nationwide anti-apartheid movement by students.

And there were the lighter moments. Janet Rice recalls that at the beginning of the year each student at TC was given a limited number of "passes" (evenings out) and what were thought of as all-important late-night passes. This meant deciding which dances/balls would be on the list. Because the Rhodes Balls (especially the Rag Ball) and their own House

Ball took precedence they had to work out carefully which Balls they wanted to attend for the year. Rag Ball was top of the list. *Mike Fuller and the Dealians* was a fabulous university band that played at almost all the Rhodes Balls and most TC Balls too. They played all the popular tunes of that time and always ended the evening with "I love Paris in the Spring Time." Everyone loved the song, but dreaded hearing the opening lines, as that heralded the end of what had (hopefully!) been a wonderful evening. The climax of the TC social calendar was the ball in Great Hall with all the girls in white evening dresses and the men in black tuxedos. Before this Sister Truda would interview each student in her office to question her about her partner. The students did not take their pleasures lightly. Everything was a great treat.

Student requests: Smoking

As early as 1933 Sister Frances Mary had made it clear just where the College stood on the matter of smoking. She stated that no smoking was allowed at College and that the authorities counted on the honour of all to accept this rule. She emphasised that they were not expressing any view as to the practice in general but that it was neither fitting nor reasonable at TC.

In August 1947 the Student Council asked whether students would be allowed to smoke at College dances. They were already allowed to do that at the leaving students' dance and at outside dances. Sister Truda agreed to this. Then in February 1948 the Council asked that the new visitors' room might be used for smoking out of College hours. The principal vetoed this request because the Insurance might be affected. In time each of the Houses was then provided with a garden arbour where the students might indulge the habit, as the Senior Student reported in 1956 "regarding happiness of students: Smoking arbours for all houses." Students of the 1960s recalled the Winchester arbour: "no smoking in your bedroom – there was a smoking arbour outside for that purpose, where those who did, smoked. It was actually quite pretty – a trellis with yellow climbing roses arched over a white wooden garden seat, where the girls would chat and puff away."

In August 1951 the students of Bangor House asked for a rain-proof shelter or for permission to use one of the music practice rooms for smoking. Only in October did the Principal reply that music rooms were not to be used for smoking. The rain-proofing of the present shelter "would be considered". Later that year, the students requested that they be allowed to smoke at the swimming bath on Sundays but Sister Truda refused saying that smoking had to be confined to the appointed smoking places and that she did not wish this extended to the swimming bath. Who was going to win this contest?

At the Student Council meeting in March 1955 it was drawn to the Principal's attention that many students smoked in the Common Room from 9.00 to 9.30 at night. Students were willing to provide their own ash trays and wash them every night. But on this the Principal remained unmoved. She reiterated that it had always been a College principle that there should be no smoking in the Hostels and she believed Insurance of Hostels was based on no fire hazards of that nature. She wished to discourage young students from smoking. If some students smoked in Common Rooms others would start the habit out of self-defence against the unpleasantness of it. The curtailment of smoking except in the quarters specially provided was a definite conviction of the Community management; and the minority of students who had acquired the habit of smoking before going to College should accept the restrictions they found there. She considered that they could do this with profit to themselves.

Student requests: Wearing of slacks

In May 1946 at the onset of cold evenings the students raised a matter which had already been aired years previously and then put to rest: they requested permission to wear slacks after supper for the evening study time. The Principal was adamant that slacks on College precincts were unnecessary and out of keeping with the dignity of an educational institution. She pointed out that the library was equipped with radiators.

A few years later the request was made again, this time with an accompanying explanation: They asked whether students could be allowed to wear slacks after Chapel in the evenings to keep warm – during winter time only – as Supper and Chapel were early giving them a chance to change before the 7.30 bell. On this matter Sister Truda was not to be moved. She would not accede to the request and considered it an important principle that informal attire should not be worn on academic premises. She reminded them that there were electric heaters in the library. She suggested that in the classrooms students would be warm enough if they wore woollen pants and knee socks.

The next year the Students Council returned to the fray but with a change to the request: Students wished to know whether they might wear slacks in the Houses over the weekends, i.e. Saturday 1pm to Sunday night. The principal replied that she was against students in residence making themselves conspicuous in their attire. It would soon seem too much effort to change for meals and she could not see that there was much benefit to be gained from wearing them in the privacy of cubicles only. They might certainly not be worn in common rooms, or gardens, or corridors.

In 1955 the students tried again asking whether during winter terms the students might wear slacks after Chapel in College only. Sister Truda replied that she thought rugs would be more suitable and convenient. After discussion at the Council meeting in March 1959, Council decided that it would be more practical if girls going to the sea on Sunday left the Hostels in slacks instead of having to change in cars or behind bushes. They asked whether the Principal agreed with this. Sister Truda and the Sisters agreed that changing in cars or behind bushes was unsuitable and so gave permission for students to leave from Hostels in slacks but insisted that they should not be seen wearing them about the College precincts or in town.

Later that year students were reminded by the Principal that slacks and shorts were not to be worn on College premises. She did not see the need for those articles of attire for dance preparations nor for clearing away on Sunday morning. By 1962 it was agreed that slacks could be worn for bicycle excursions out of town and the next year students were given permission to wear slacks in College grounds at certain times including prep at night. Thus ended the war of the slacks!

Sartorial suitability and dress rules

An annual sartorial suitability lecture had long featured on the TC calendar. This had been introduced by Sister Frances Mary in the hope that it would raise the level of students' care and neatness in dress which had been adversely commented upon by some townspeople. Hazel Jandrell (Marillier) (1941–1942) recalling her years as a student remembered that all first years had to attend a lecture on sartorial suitability. She said it was interesting and drew attention to another responsibility of teachers. She was a student during the War years when they were allowed not to wear stockings on campus but out of the grounds they had to wear stockings. In those years the students wore overalls and stockings for teaching. The College dress code had to be observed. Among her recollections was that they had to wear a blue tunic for eurhythmics which was before breakfast and they had to wear their overalls over their tunics for breakfast. They wore gym dress and black stockings for gym. They wore dresses for the evening meal when they could smarten up with jewellery.

A few years later Edith Blackbeard (Judge) (1944–1947) repeated that rules were strict. Dresses had to be a certain length; hats and stockings had to be worn out of the gate. Boyfriends were carefully screened and, in some cases interviewed by Sister Frances Mary herself.

An OG of the 1950s wrote: "To make sure we did not disgrace our College, we had to watch a sartorial suitability parade. No slacks were allowed, and we wore hats to church on Sunday nights. For gym we wore blue blouses and short blue skirts. When going to teach gym at a school we had to wear longer skirts over our short ones. For life-saving we duck-dived for bricks wearing skirts, blouses and tackies." These students were being prepared for a profession and training in every respect was taken seriously.

College dances

Much the same approach was evident in the matter of College dances. A student of the 1930s, Enid Mills, recalled that for House dances they had a programme and a pencil. The student's partner was allowed only three dances. The rest of the dances were claimed by men they exchanged glances with while the band had its break.

An undated hand-written note by Sister Truda states that College dances were still considered to be formal College functions. They were made so in the hope that this would raise the standard of behaviour. Printed invitation cards were sent out in the name of the College. It was expected that these would be acknowledged formally by the guests invited by the students as their partners. The students were responsible for ensuring that acceptances reached the Principal in good time. If for some reason an acceptance did not arrive before the evening of the dance the student concerned had to take her partner to the Principal's office to introduce him. There were to be no last minute arrangements.

At a Student Council Meeting in 1952 the Principal noted that the custom of introducing partners to host and hostess at College Dances had lapsed. She felt that it was a desirable courtesy and that familiarity with correct forms helped to give social ease and poise. The Principal in true TC fashion felt that this was a valuable lesson for teachers in training who at some time in the future could well find themselves organising school dances. Clearly the whole time at the College was seen as a learning curve. The Principal decried the use of what she termed "undesirable Americanisms" when students introduced gentleman friends to her.

Much later (about 1970) new regulations concerning invitations were issued in what appears to be Mrs Craig's handwriting. All that was then required was that the name of the student and that of her partner should be given to the student from whom the dance ticket was purchased. How times had changed!

Subject rooms, experimentation and examinations

In the College Log Book this entry appears in the First Quarter 1937: "Establishment of subject rooms in place of classrooms." TC was experimenting briefly with the Dalton Method of teaching. It involved a radical change of system with the drawback of congestion and consequent untidiness and disorder. TC was in the vanguard of experimentation, enthusiastically encouraged by the Inspectors.

By 1951 the Principal was wondering whether the College was in fact still in the vanguard as it had been under Sister Frances Mary. Sister Truda had been Assistant to Sister Frances Mary in all the new projects. She considered that the College had spent a long time consolidating the rapid advances of that period. She was conscious of the College having lost ground and wondered whether they had given in too easily to the obstacles to sound experimentation which they were experiencing at that time.

In 1953 Sister Truda reported to the Board that in instruction given to the students caution and discretion were urged in applying activity methods. Later that year she commented: "We have not been able to go as far in this experiment of Activity Methods as we wished...in keeping with the tendency overseas which is towards modified activity methods; retaining always the drills and firm grounding in basic subjects; not throwing the timetables out of the window as was first advocated but using the stimulus of activity methods to bring a thrill into lessons..." And so was abandoned the subject-room plan "which savoured of a Dalton regime which we do not use" and the original classroom system was reinstated.

Following a spate of cheating, the Assignment System had fallen into disfavour and so in 1961 the College returned to the Exam System. In the Inspectors' Report it was laid down that examinations would carry two-thirds of the marks and the College record only one-third of final assessment. The Assignment System was a most valuable method of study and the Inspectors hoped that it would not be crowded out altogether. The Principal commented that there was not enough time!

The students were taken aback by this change. The prospect of mid-year examinations and June Reports based on them which were to be used as testimonials in applying for posts caused considerable unrest. The Principal seemed undaunted: "we seem to have weathered that..." The students bounced back and made the best of the situation although with mixed feelings. They were not accustomed to lengthy examinations.

The staff considered that assignment work and current tests produced a better standard of work. They felt that examinations turned the clock back. The students had immediately returned to their high school habits of just turning on the tap at the mention of a stimulus word and producing everything in their notebooks which had anything to do with the stimulus word but not necessarily with any relation to the question set.

Administrative problems and the appointment of a male Bursar

The Log Book records that on 26 April 1959 Sister Mary Eleanor was withdrawn from the Bursar's Office to become Assistant Superior. Mrs

Norman Taylor had been appointed College Bursar from 1 June 1959 and Miss Clayton would act as Bursar during the month of May. Sister Paulina was then appointed as Assistant Bursar. The College had managed for 66 years with a Sister-Bursar, but the work had grown considerably over the years and it needed a properly qualified book-keeper.

A sub-committee of the Advisory Board was appointed to consider difficulties that had arisen in the College administration. The matters dealt with included Finance, Household, Grounds and Maintenance Staff, and Office Staff. The Chairman of the sub-committee was the Dean of Grahamstown, the Very Revd John Hodson. Financially the College was not in a strong position and much stringency was required. TC was a large institution. At that time, July 1960, the total cost of Household, Outdoor, and Office Staff, was just over £10 000 p.a. The Board had to consider whether it was getting the most efficient and economic return for this heavy outlay.

The household department appeared to be running smoothly and economically though the College was large, and the Hostels widely separated. Where the ground and maintenance staff were concerned, there were two foremen working quite independently with no common supervision of their work. When she was Bursar, Sister Mary Eleanor supervised the foremen; that was clearly something that lapsed when Mrs Taylor was appointed. It was in the Bursar's Office that the difficulty lay. The sub-committee felt that while Sister Truda was Principal and had everything at her fingertips all would be well. It would be unreasonable to expect a new incumbent to be responsible for both the administration of the College's educational work and its management. Clearly what was needed was a person who would take over the whole load of management from the principal.

The Committee discussed the possibility of a male Bursar who would be responsible for keeping all the accounts, receiving all the fees and paying all the bills. He would also be responsible for the estate and would supervise the two foremen and other ground staff and see to the fabric of the whole property. Additional duties would include being responsible for seeing that the catering arrangements, buying, and related matters, were carried out as well and as economically as possible. It would be his responsibility to make quarterly reports to the Board and to be present at their meetings until after the Financial Report had been tabled.

The burning question here was to whom the Bursar would be answerable. Dr Thomas Alty of Rhodes University offered the answer. He wrote to Sister Truda that it should be laid down without any doubt that the Principal had the final responsibility and that the bursar should take his instructions from her. If that was made clear, he thought that almost anything else would work.

Once again, the duality of the situation came to the fore. Sister Truda put this well: "The principal must, of necessity, keep in close touch with the finances of the college. As Sister in Charge of a community work, she is responsible to the Superior of the Community and the Community Chapter, and a male bursar could not take this off her, but only ease the burden of daily administrative work and supervision of estate staff... The principal, through the manager, is responsible to the Education Department for our grant-aided finances and this too, she must continue to supervise." The Board encouraged the appointment of a male Bursar and Mr Eddie Whitford was duly appointed, being the first man to be appointed to the actual College staff albeit on the administrative side.

Another administrative problem: Departmental interference?

The Community Sisters were protective of "their" Training College. A request from the Department received during 1961 for representation on the College Advisory Board threw them into a panic. They felt extremely apprehensive about the implications of such a request. As a result of their representations the Department withdrew its request and instead asked for the formation of an Advisory Committee.

It must be remembered that TC was an aided Training College of the Cape Provincial Administration but that its management and maintenance was vested in the recognised manager who performed the functions of a committee (she was empowered to take decisions without consultation) and was responsible directly to the Department. (Ordinance No 20 of 1956, Paragraph 71 (i)). The manager of the College was the elected Superior of the Community of the Resurrection of Our Lord which was itself the owner of the College. The Manager was assisted in her responsibilities by an Advisory Board of approximately twelve members. They were invited by the Manager to serve on the Board for an indefinite period. The Manager also invited one member of the Board to be its Chairman.

So in 1961 the Education Department requested that an Advisory Committee be set up in addition to the Board already mentioned. This was to consist of a chairman and six members; the Chairman and three members were to be invited by the Manager, and three members nominated by the SGE. This gave the Education Department direct representation on the Committee which was there to advise the Manager in her conduct of the College notably in the appointment of staff. Both Advisory Board and Advisory Committee were advisory to the Manager and the Manager was responsible directly to the Department. The SGE assured the Sisters that in selecting members of the proposed committee the Department would certainly bear in mind the custom of the College of inviting persons who were practising members of one or other Christian denomination.

The request of the SGE was brought to a Community Chapter and the Minutes reveal that the Sisters felt threatened by this innovation wondering how they would safeguard the principles for which the College stood. The College was almost entirely residential and was administered as a unit and it was only the close co-operation of Sisters in residences which made possible the smooth running of such a large unit under the final authority of the Principal. The Department had always expressed itself as most grateful to the Sisters and they were therefore confident that they would continue to receive the same support and encouragement from the Advisory Committee.

Historically TC's relations with the SGE and with the Chief Inspector of the Cape Education Department had always been most cordial. They had been of a personal nature following the example of Mother Cecile and Dr Muir. The Manager had always been able to call on the advice of people with a close and intimate knowledge of the working of the Education Department and the Cape Administration. But by then members of the Community were apprehensive as to whether those friendly relations would continue under the existing Government because the SGE was under the direction of the Administrator of the Cape Province, the latter being a political appointment.

At the Annual Chapter in January 1962 a Motion proposed by Sister Truda and seconded by Sister Virginia read: "Bearing in mind the expressed wish and intentions of our Foundress, Mother Cecile, to work in the closest co-operation with the Education Authorities, and also the respect and consideration the Education Department has always shown towards the particular aims and ideals of this Training College, this Chapter expresses its readiness to agree to the SG's request for the establishment of an Advisory Committee to the Manager on which the Education Department should be directly represented in the proportion of three Departmental nominees to four nominees of the College, the Chairman being nominated by the Manager, and the Principal being present at all Meetings of the said Committee and the Manager being present at her discretion."

Speaking to the Motion Sister Virginia felt that their only course was to accept with a good grace what they could not avoid and to pray that they would be given wisdom and grace to continue the task God had given them of owning and administering their Aided Training Institution of the Cape Education Department even in the changed conditions of having a

Government party in power with which they did not feel much sympathy and from whom they feared unwelcome interference. On being put to the vote the motion was carried: *Nem Con*. One of the appointees of the SGE was Professor Gerber of the Education Faculty at Rhodes University. He wrote reassuringly to the Manager that he had been in Grahamstown and associated with education in almost all its aspects long enough to realise and appreciate the emphases of the College. He would not like to see it change. What he would like was to see the academic qualifications of the staff increasingly stepped up bearing in mind the religious affiliations of the College.

Improvements to campus under Sister Truda

Winchester House

Winchester House, an old colonial house on the corner of Somerset and Grey Streets, just over the road from the main College building had been purchased in 1924 as a suitable residence for single lay staff. The drawback was that any teacher living there was expected to assist with evening duties. Furthermore, the residents found themselves isolated from people living in the town. In the end it was agreed that it was better for staff to find accommodation in the town where they would find congenial company for out-of-College hours. The house was then used for various purposes, including as the sanatorium.

By 1945 following the slump experienced during the War, numbers at the Training Colleges were picking up. The Rhodesian government had also decided to send students to college in Grahamstown. Further residential accommodation was necessary. The Principal wrote to Mr Steer the Editor of the East London *Daily Despatch* and Secretary of the Crewe Trust. This was obviously an appeal for funds towards further building. She needed money to build a new hostel for the Training College students. The original hostels provided sleeping accommodation in small cubicles. These now needed to be remodelled thus reducing the available accommodation and therefore another hostel would be necessary. The University in such proximity to the College provided attractive study-bedrooms and this fact added to the problem by showing TC accommodation in an unfavourable light. Mr Steer could not assist at that time but later several donations were received from the Crewe Trust.

In October 1949 Sister Truda spoke to the Community about the need for extra accommodation for the numbers anticipated in 1950. Attention focussed on Winchester. There was a two-fold plan: first, to build an extension, and later, to add a further storey. What was envisaged was first a new wing of ten rooms and bathrooms to be added behind Winchester.

The new building would be joined to Winchester by a covered way. The contract price including hot water and electricity was estimated at £3750. The Mother said there was £2000 available in the bank at that time. Fifty to sixty Rhodesian students were expected the following year and a *per caput* grant paid by the Rhodesian Government for these students would largely meet the cost. It was thought better to spend the money on enlarging the College premises than on renting houses. On inspection the old house was found to be not in a condition to support an upper storey, so it was back to the drawing board.

It was then decided to demolish the old house and build a new Hostel on that site at the cost of £10 000. It was suggested that the grant of £12-10-0 per head per annum for the 50–60 Rhodesian students should be used to pay off a loan. A loan of £9000 was negotiated from the Standard Bank. The overdraft would be renewed annually for nine years being decreased at the rate of £1000 per year. The Art School, now the Carinus Art Centre, owned by the Community had been let for £25 per month and that rental would pay the interest on the loan. The new building would take five months to complete. To economise on staffing the College authorities decided to have only the four houses: Canterbury, Lincoln, Bangor and Winchester.

As an illustration of the hand-to-mouth financial exigencies of the College, Sister Truda suggested in May 1959 that Chapter should think seriously of selling the Art School and using the money for the renovation of the existing hostels to bring them into line with the Government-owned hostels. The property had been valued at £8490. She pointed out that the low rate of interest charged by the Community on loans made to the College obscured the real cost of running the College.

By the mid-1960s it was felt necessary to extend the new Winchester House by the addition of an extra wing. Hitherto some students had been housed at Salisbury House in Donkin Street, but it was some distance from the College which resulted in frequent disciplinary troubles. In addition, it was uneconomical to run. The planned extension to Winchester would provide additional accommodation for eighteen students and would cost over £5000. It would include a new large Common Room. The old Common Room would become a Students' Visitors' Room which was badly needed. This would be ready by January 1961. The College Advisory Board was in favour of this and the members were satisfied that the cost could be covered within the next few years.

The need for modernisation

There was real anxiety concerning the upgrading of the Hostels. It inevitably involved the College in further debt. But there was no possibility of applying for building grants from the Cape Education Department as that would mean handing over the Hostels to be administered by the Department. The Community could not contemplate such a move.

In a letter appealing for funds the Superior wrote that as the residential system had always been a feature of the College they were extremely reluctant to hand over Hostels to the Department. At the same time as providing optimum facilities for the professional training of students they had always aimed at using their strong residential system as a means of amplifying the professional training with all-round character building. It was precisely this aspect of the College's work combined with professional training of a high standard which was so greatly valued. Three of the Hostels, Canterbury 1907, Lincoln/Westminster 1913 and Bangor 1923 dated back to the days of the small cubicles which were decidedly *outré* and needed to be changed hence the need to spend money on them. Winchester dated from 1950 and was satisfactory.

It was felt, with some justification, that TC was rendering an important service to the State and that educational work should be financed by public taxation. The Superior was satisfied that the College should apply for and accept the full benefit of the Grant allowed by Ordinance to Aided Training Institutions without sacrificing any of its independence. A request was made in terms of the Ordinance of 1921 for a maintenance grant for TC. The Superior went so far as to say that the College was living on its reputation and that they should improve their accommodation which was below the standard of new Government training college hostels.

It is relevant to note what was happening at the Government colleges. The SGE in his report for 1962 had ascribed the fall-off in applicants for teacher training to the inadequate and often unattractive accommodation not only at the teaching buildings but also at the hostels. New buildings had been erected at Paarl, Wellington and Cape Town, and were then in the process of being erected at Graaff-Reinet and Oudtshoorn. Approval was given for new buildings or extensions for Cape Town and Denneoord in Stellenbosch. The SGE was pleased to report that new hostels had been built at all the colleges and at most of them the old hostels had been extended and renovated. The magnitude of the programme can be seen by the money spent on the colleges, (Expenditure March 1957–March 1962) – see overleaf.

	College	Hostels	Total
Graaff-Reinet	R37 250.59	R34 443.40	R71 693.99
Paarl	R263 382.85	R298 668.95	R562 057.80
Wellington	R234 135.62	R287 596.75	R521 732.37
Oudtshoorn	R1 360.00	R188 110.40	R189 470.40
Cape Town	R26 344.84	R198 183.93	R224 528.13
Stellenbosch	R46 476.84	R255 235.50	R301 712.34

Compared with these figures the outlay at TC appears to be modest. The SGE considered that when the works in hand and those projected including the erection of another training college (in Port Elizabeth) had been completed, the Department would be in a better position to provide teacher training facilities commensurate with modern requirements and the needs of its schools.

A general look at College finances: Students' fees

Financially TC was never out of the woods. Until 1924 the financial affairs of the College and the Community were treated as one. After that date a separation was made. A recurring problem in the College was the arrears in fees. The authorities were hesitant about adopting the rigorous methods of some secular institutions to ensure payment. The financial position was not good and so the Finance Committee issued a directive in 1931 on the need to forego all unnecessary expenses.

Again in 1934 it was agreed that any expenditure should be carefully watched. The Bursar reported that the College account was overdrawn at the bank. A month later she reported that the overdraft had been paid but that fees were coming in slowly. The dilemma facing the Sisters over outstanding fees was that they felt they should approach the matter in a Christian and charitable way. It was always a hand-to-mouth existence for the College. In July 1934 for example the account was overdrawn because of the non-payment of Government loans for first-year students amounting to £345 and the heavy expenses incurred during the second term.

These examples show how the situation was handled: In 1926 the debt owed by a leaving student stood at £131.17.6d. It was felt that this was too heavy a debt to send a girl out with. It was decided that she should only be asked to pay back £80, but that it should be put to her that if she could refund more she ought to do so. A year later another unpaid account amounting to £64.15.5 was discussed. It was agreed to reduce it by £14.15.5, leaving a total of £50 to be paid. In June 1930 the Bursar asked if an account amounting to £28.9.0 could be written off. The last daughter had left College in June 1927 and the family was in great financial difficulties. The Committee agreed on condition that if the father's circumstances improved he should then send what he could.

At a later meeting that year the Bursar asked what steps should be taken about the arrears owing from several past students. It was decided she should go to see Mr Gill of the Board of Executors (BOE) and ask his advice about taking further steps to procure the payments. On another account it was felt that a summons should be issued as no payment had been made for some time and the debtor had not replied to letters requesting payment. In the case of another account the Bursar mentioned that those people only made a payment when pressed to do so by the Albany BOE. In this instance it was agreed to reduce the account by half providing a settlement was made immediately in one payment. No payment was expected on another account because of losses on the farm but as that family had always paid up-to-date it was agreed that the student should be granted a College loan of £30. In the case of another parent the Albany Board of the BOE asked whether they might threaten him with arrest without the College's name appearing. After discussion it was decided to leave the matter and write off the account as a bad debt.

The perilous nature of the finances: An overview

To illustrate just how tight finances were, in June 1938 the Finance Committee discussed the purchase of an HMV radio-gramophone for £45. This expenditure was not considered justified. Later Sister Frances Mary raised the matter of buying a film projector as the staff was anxious to ensure that students leaving TC were familiar with up-to-date equipment, but it was decided that the expense was too heavy to incur at that time in view of the Building Fund.

The early 1940s saw the College finances at such a low ebb that it is perhaps pertinent to ask just how the College managed to survive. In September 1942 the Bursar requested permission to have the College Overdraft Facility raised from £1500 to £2000. By October the overdraft stood at just below the agreed amount, but further sums were needed to cover current expenses incurred in the building programme. It was eventually agreed that £500 of Community money would be withdrawn from the savings bank and lent to the College. By November there was no longer an overdraft, but no accounts had been paid! It was expected that the overdraft would climb to £2000 yet again. Furthermore £2100 was now owed by the College to the Community but repayment had not been asked for yet.

The situation was so precarious that in January 1944 it was proposed that the College should be further assisted in its financial difficulty by the

Community. This seemed to be the recurrent story where TC was concerned. By November 1945 the Bursar said the College finances were better as the fees had been received but no bills had been paid. The housekeeping had been reduced by £500 the previous quarter through greater supervision. The money lent by the Community had helped to reduce the overdraft. The fact that enrolment in all the training colleges was down due partly to the war situation added to the problem. In the meantime, boarding fees had gone up to £15.15.0 per quarter but by the start of the new year in 1946 Sister Frances Mary reported that some of the parents were finding it difficult to meet the increased fees. It was agreed to offer boarding bursaries to the value of £10 per annum. After being encouraged to do so the College applied to the Department of Education for a rent-grant to cover interest on building loans

During the post-War years the College was gradually slipping out of the Sisters' grasp. The fact that there were so few teaching Sisters perhaps accounts for this. The Community was not attracting as many recruits as previously. There had been many changes in the world following two world wars. The Mother said more than once at Chapter that the postulants who had come since the War (1914-1918) with all the changes that had brought into modern life were different from those who came before the War...

As early as 1927 there was a serious shortage of teaching Sisters for the various works in which the Community was involved in addition to TC. When Sister Virginia resigned from the Principalship in 1969, for the first time in the history of the Community there were no novices. There was increasing difficulty in staffing the Community works owing to the reduction in numbers of those able to do active work. The residential accommodation at TC had always been run by the Sisters. That was no longer possible and lay members of staff were appointed. This aggravated the financial situation as these women had to be paid.

The Grahamstown Training College eventually closed its doors, but Rhodes University had bought the college campus for extensions to the University. The first instalment of R150 000 received in January 1974 was invested to provide income for the Community as their funds were low. The second instalment was expected in January 1975 and the Superior informed the Community that about R22 000 of that payment would be used to liquidate the College overdraft at the Standard Bank. The Community had been obliged to borrow from investments and that amount would have to be repaid. With closure imminent, the College was having a bad time financially because of the reduction in numbers. The payments were received just in time to avoid a dire situation financially where both College and Community were concerned.

The Music School post-1945

The Training College continued to uphold its reputation in the field of music. The Founder's Day Concert on 14 November 1953 was reviewed in *Grocott's Mail* by Dr Patrick Wise. He spoke of this being one of the events that many Grahamstonians looked forward to with intense pleasure. The programme commenced with orchestral pieces followed by a choir of second-year students and then the Senior College Choir singing most effectively unaccompanied. He praised the standard of this concert which he felt augured well for the future of the TC School of Music.

At the Founder's Day Concert the following year, Dr Wise referred to solo-singing rendered with that clarity of diction which was a feature of TC work. He praised a performance which was full of little touches of imaginative and sensitive musicianship implanted by Mr Kirby who obtained wonderfully responsive singing from a choir able to dispense with their copies and thus give all their attention to the conductor.

Mr Iliffe-Higgo had retired in 1952 after completing 32 years of service to TC Music School. During his time at TC he had sent out 120 trained music teachers with the UTLM qualification into the schools of the country. He had also prepared students for the Performer's Licentiate. This Licentiate instruction had taken place in Mr Iliffe-Higgo's spare time in addition to his responsibilities as a departmental piano teacher. He was remembered as a teacher who took a personal interest in his students. In his place Mr Kirby was to conduct the orchestra for concerts and musical evenings.

Sister Margery who had taught Class Music also retired at this time. She was an OG who had been at TC since 1917, had an LRAM in Harmony, was a House Sister, and was particularly remembered for her excellent leadership in Chapel Choir and Junior Choir.

In 1954 Sister Truda wrote to Mr Kirby to confirm that the orchestra would lapse as a regular feature and that he would organise it as an extramural activity when he required it for any special occasion. Attitudes were changing. In October 1956 the students made it clear that they were not prepared to give up their free evenings to attend rehearsals for the operetta *Papageno*, from Mozart's opera *The Magic Flute*. The students wanted to enjoy their free evenings rather than fulfil an obligation. Sister Truda agreed to have a word with the cast and discuss the matter with them. The show had to go on and the operetta was performed in the City Hall on Founder's Day. It was a kaleidoscope of colour and movement. The City Hall was chosen because the Memorial Hall did not allow for the freedom of movement necessary for producing the operetta.

The Music School had always been a private enterprise on the part of the Training College. The College existed for the training of primary school teachers and as far as the Cape Education Department was concerned the teaching of instrumentalists was entirely extraneous to the ordinary curriculum expected in a training college. The College did not set out to train specialist instrumental music teachers. By 1959 the general lack of musical talent in the College, added to the fact that there were no longer any full-time music students, left the music staff with only the departmental students from whom to draw for a concert.

Why had this collapse of the Music School happened? The Music Department at Rhodes University had been established in 1923 and though described by Mr R F Currey in his *Rhodes University 1904–1970* as the "Cinderella of Rhodes departments", by the 1950s it had taken off and students were then able to take a degree which would qualify them to teach music. This had an adverse effect on enrolment at the Music School at TC.

Since its inception in 1903 the Music School had brought honour and popularity to TC. It had also done excellent pioneer work in musical education. By May 1947 it was not on a sound financial basis. The Sisters could not afford to offer high salaries to attract highly qualified specialists. So in 1949 the Music School was officially incorporated into TC for the education of departmental teachers-in-training.

The College authorities would continue to employ teachers of solo-singing and stringed instruments in a private capacity if they were able to get them. The staff of the Music School wherever possible would also continue to train specialist music teachers. As from January 1949 the Cape Education Department created two music teacher posts at TC. Further, in the new curriculum for training colleges, Class Music was made an optional subject where previously it had been compulsory. This in turn affected the number of students learning the piano. The staff of the Music School agreed that it was certainly wiser for those who took Class Music to have piano lessons where they had the advantage of aural training and scales.

The new regulations appeared to suggest that choirs were no longer to be compulsory, but the staff decided that at TC for those students who chose to take Class Music, choir would be compulsory as there was great value to be gained and that any student wishing to belong to a choir could do so as an extramural activity. It was decided to make piano or singing lessons compulsory for students taking Class Music.

Contrary to all expectation the number of students choosing Class Music rose and the numbers continued to grow. In 1962 there were 190 in all including the large IST class. Sister Kathleen Mary who taught Class Music was credited with having attracted these numbers. The linking of Class Music to the piano had also played a part. The larger numbers brought other problems. No one teacher could cope adequately with the testing involved.

Several of the Sisters were involved with the Music School or the Orchestra over the years. Sister Katherine Maud played in the Orchestra. Sister Gertrude Bridget taught for a time in the Music School and was also a member of the Orchestra where she played the violin. She had a special gift of music, and teaching it theoretically and practically on piano and violin was her main occupation. Sister Ethel Agnes, greatly gifted as a musician, was also on the staff of the Music School. Sister Emily, a violinist, was regarded as having laid the foundations of the College Orchestra, for she herself was musical and was enthusiastic in her encouragement of others. Sister Ada Mary played the piano and for a time was 'cellist in the College Orchestra. She had taught music before joining the Community and was occasionally organist in St Mary's Chapel. Sister Margery and Sister Kathleen Mary have already been mentioned.

When the orchestra was disbanded it was decided to sell the orchestral equipment belonging to the College. The proceeds would go towards the fund for a new organ for the Chapel.

The Old Girls' Guilds in the latter years

When the decision was taken in 1957 to hold the Reunion on Founder's Day it was decided to make more use of the local group meetings in different centres as OGs were no longer able or willing to travel to Grahamstown.

The opinions of the OGs mattered because of the strong OG Guilds throughout the country which remained closely linked with the Sisters particularly. It was through the OGs that the College was made widely known. The College was a Community foundation with a strong Christian intention and tradition. It was understood that branches should not only keep OGs in touch, but also that each branch would provide a group to which students leaving College could be referred. TC also needed the interest and support of the OGs. This two-way loving care and interest could only be achieved by close contact between the College and the Branches.

There was a Guild Rule:
- To make a constant effort to continue steadfast in all good things learned while at College
- To pray for the work of the Sisters of St Peter's Home, and all their helpers and for fellow members of the Guild.
- To endeavour to keep in touch with the Sisters by occasional correspondence.
- To attend, where possible, the Reunion of the Guild.
- To remember to pay the Annual subscription.

The reverse side of the Card gave Counsel to members:
- The Members are earnestly entreated while passing through the things of *Time*, to keep in remembrance the things that are unseen and *Eternal*.
- They are reminded of the importance of maintaining, at any cost, their personal union with Him, who says: Apart from ME you can do nothing.
- To this end they are urged to be faithful in keeping a simple Rule about Prayer, Bible Reading, Holy Communion and some definite work for Christ.
- They are also affectionately invited to communicate with College in any time of difficulty or trouble.

The College closed in 1975 but the OGs have continued their meetings although their numbers are gradually declining. The author has had opportunities to attend such Branch Meetings where those present are happy to recall their days at College. The Annual Publication which is sent out *Grahamstown Training College: News and Views* has until recently been prepared by OG Mrs Astrid Gorvett and contains interesting reminiscences plus reports of meetings held at various places. The *TC: News and Views* 2008 gives reports on the Guilds in Port Elizabeth, Cape Town, Johannesburg, KZN Midlands, Port Alfred, Harare, Grahamstown and East London. The *TC: News and Views* 2012 includes in addition Graaff-Reinet, Durban and the Natal South Coast.

The Editorial by Pam Creach in *The Vocal Discord* for November 1971 expressed the thoughts of generations of OGs: "I have heard remarks from 3rd year students recently that they subconsciously walk around College and Grahamstown with absorbent eyes in order to store memories that no doubt will bring many a smile to Old Students when discussing their years at this college...for 3 years...so many experiences shared, people from different walks of life brought together, only to be scattered again..."

CHAPTER 7

TC under Sister Virginia
1962–1969

LIKE HER PREDECESSOR, Sister Virginia (Miss Nonie Newey – "Virge" to the students) was from the Eastern Cape having been born on the family farm near East London. She was an OG and one of the students who benefitted from the arrangement made by Sister Truda and the Superior with the Rhodes University authorities. For a four-year experimental period, Rhodes agreed to accept the two-year Primary Teachers' Course as exemption from the first year of a B.A. degree course at Rhodes University. On completion of the PT Course, College students with a Matriculation Certificate or its equivalent might apply for exemption from four of the following six first-year Degree Courses if they had taken these subjects for two years at the Training College: English, Afrikaans-Nederlands, History, Bible Studies, Art, Physical Education with Hygiene. If there were subjects among these in which they would like to major, then they could proceed at once to second year courses, and so complete a degree in two years. Sister Virginia took that route majoring in Biblical Studies and Theology (the latter a two-year major course).

Panel inspections

From 4 to 6 May 1964 the College was subjected to a Panel Inspection. The Inspectors once again congratulated the College on the quality of its work and the maintenance of the high standards it had always set. They commented on the pleasant, wholesome and happy atmosphere and the evidence of well-directed and purposeful activity. The Inspectors were impressed by the extensive use made of the library and heartily approved of the assignment system which they considered to be the outstanding feature of the College although by then it was continued in a restricted way. TC had proved the value of this system and consequently the Department was keen to promote it elsewhere. They commended the English teaching which aimed to enrich the literary background of students and to train them in the art of bringing life to teaching of language work in the classroom in addition to instilling basic accuracy in written and spoken language.

The next Panel Inspection took place in June 1966. The Inspectors commented on the excellent planning of the work and the whole organisation of the College. Once again, they were impressed by the high standards and the emphasis placed on individual activity by students. They praised the excellent use made of the library and of the place of the Chapel in setting the tone for which the College was renowned. The three lecturers in English appeared competent and thorough in their teaching.

At the time of the 1966 Panel Inspection Sister Virginia discussed academic standards with the Inspectors. She felt there was too much emphasis on practical activities to the detriment of the essential academic work, particularly the languages. The Inspectors stated that it was noticeable in all the Colleges that the present-day students were not as well equipped academically as they had been in previous years. More work had to be done at the College to bring students up to the necessary standard by the end of the two-year course.

The Principal was emphatic that the College authorities would rather maintain the existing high standards with a slightly smaller enrolment than produce a huge batch of indifferent teachers. The policy of the College all along had been to weed out unsuitable students from as early in the first year as possible. She was also strongly opposed to the idea that the third year of the primary course should move in the direction of specialisation. What was really needed in the Primary School was the competent class-teacher.

The SGE Report for 1962 had emphasised that the Department felt the need for a radical improvement in the training of its teachers and looked forward to the day when a minimum three-year period of training would be required for all primary teachers. The demands of modern society made it imperative that the teachers should be better equipped than those of a generation previously. By 1963 a compulsory three-year course was an imminent possibility

In 1966 enrolment at the College was the highest ever with 277 students. The ever-present problems manifested themselves yet again: discipline and rules, Chapel attendance, leave facilities. The possibility of third-year students going into private boarding was considered. The Principal reported on the continual agitation among some of the third-year students for more freedom from residential restrictions. She considered they had enough freedom in this respect, a great deal more than in some of the other Colleges (e.g. at Graaff-Reinet where third-year students were allowed one late-night pass per week – late meaning 9.00 p.m.) An OG recalled that they always felt like the "poor cousins" compared with the Rhodes girls – the TC girls had to be in at 11.00 on Saturday or 12 after a dance while Rhodes girls had 1 a.m. as their curfew. But that was the rule and so be it!

The dilemma faced by the Sisters remained the same: how to maintain, without compromise, the essential principles and ideals and standards for which TC stood? It appeared that much that had been taken for granted in the past was outside the experience of the students then in College. Sister Virginia included in this for instance courtesy towards adults in general. She felt that students needed to be told things which one would have assumed they would have been doing all their lives. She was encouraged when she heard from people totally unconnected with the College that they appreciated the better standards of behaviour which they encountered among their students in general as compared with that which they encountered in young people of the same age from other environments. The staff at TC was always conscious of the fact that qualified students leaving the College were the public face of the Institution.

Facing challenges

Sister Virginia was aware that the College could not allow itself to settle into a rut. Every new challenge had to be met as it arose: the challenges of new teaching techniques, of social change, and of student demands. The aim was always to equip the students with the best training which would enable them to meet successfully the challenges not only of life as a whole but also of their professional life.

The change in teaching techniques included the whole new field of audio-visual equipment. Writing to the OGs, Sister Virginia commented that this was a fascinating field for experiment. The enterprising teacher could make endless use of the various types of audio-visual aids that were becoming available. She was looking forward to the Department being able to supply TC as promised with several strip projectors, more than one ciné projector and two or three record players. The members of staff were learning the new techniques so that they could train the students.

The College attempted to teach the students how to take their place confidently as independent young women in society after leaving College. An OG of 1965–1966 admitted that she realised later that she belonged to an association of dedicated teachers with a wonderful outlook on life. She said that this might not have been of great interest to her while at College, as she was too busy getting on with it. As one matured one's perspective changed, and one had more time to think. That the Sisters and staff managed to achieve this may be gauged from the high reputation in which the College was held throughout the country and elsewhere. An OG of 1973–1975 recognised this, saying that there was no doubt that there was something about their Training College that worked. There were lots of things that the students rebelled against, but TC trained them thoroughly in their profession as well as maintaining certain standards and life skills.

By 1969 the Sisters were realising that young people at that time were coming from different homes and backgrounds and were completely unused to discipline. Many were independent even in their teens and had a generally questioning attitude.

Students and Hostel/College Rules

Over the years the responsibility of keeping adequate control of the Hostels in the evening had become ever more acute. The difficulty increased as boy-friends became more numerous and persistent and as the students became more inclined to disregard rules about study-hours and leave-nights. Pitted against this were the high principles espoused by the Sisters in their running of the College. Clearly the time had come when the day to day management and control of student activities should be the responsibility of the senior students. To this end House Committees were introduced along the same lines as those in the women's residences at Rhodes University.

There was a second matter which really appalled both staff and Sisters. There had been for some time a great deal of deceit and dishonesty among the students in the hostels regarding social activities. Lying and cheating appeared to be extensive and increasing. They found this quite deplorable in any circumstances and especially so in young women who were going out to teach children. The authorities acknowledged that many of the rules were restricting and chafing and felt they could re-design them to remove many of the irritating points and to try to eliminate the practice of lying and cheating. They hoped that the students would in future conduct their lives on a more honest basis; and that those who were naturally honest would find the rules less irksome.

Sister Virginia agonised over what rules should be applied, especially in the hostels. She realised the danger of seeming anachronistically rigid but believed that the students needed a good deal of guidance and protection. She commented that they were not nearly as knowledgeable as they liked to think they were.

One of the changes was that compulsory evening Chapel for all students was dropped. Another was that the Bishop of Grahamstown gave permission for non-Anglicans to receive the sacrament in the College Chapel and, on the instigation of the Roman Catholic priest, in future Roman Catholic students were to attend Morning Prayers and also take the Scripture course. The winds of change emanating from the Second Vatican Council in Rome had reached Grahamstown!

The Sisters were finding the degree of resistance to the rule concerning Chapel and Worship most disconcerting. They considered making compliance a condition of acceptance at the College. Sister Virginia felt that it was hypocritical of students to ask for training at TC in preference to that of other colleges while having no intention of conforming to TC customs. For Sister Virginia all this added considerably to the pressures of running the College.

Staffing problems: Enter male lecturers...

Problems of staffing the College continued to be a matter of concern, as they had been since the war. There were no teaching Sisters available, hence the critical staffing situation. A suggestion came from the inspectorate that they should advertise vacant posts – even the permanent positions – for male or female applicants. It might be possible to appoint on probation suitable men, married and recommended by their inspectors.

Acting on this suggestion the manager received permission from the Department to advertise for teachers of either sex. In November 1963 Sister Virginia reported that 12 out of 13 applications had been from men. Mr JC Knox who had applied for the Geography post was duly appointed to the permanent staff. Later Mr Harry Hare-Bowers was appointed Afrikaans lecturer. In 1959 the staff had numbered 25 of whom five were Sisters and one was a man (at the Music School). By 1965 out of 25 staff there were four Sisters and six men and in 1971 the staff of 25 included one Sister and seven men.

The male teachers were well received by the students. There had been men in the Music School from the earliest years and the staff readily adjusted. An OG recalls that Mr Sadler treated the students like real adults – he taught them that you could not hope to teach every lesson one-hundred percent every day but that they should aim at teaching one brilliant lesson daily. There was Mr Webster the science boffin, Mr Knox who taught them about "tall grass, scattered trees and boooshes" and Mr Harry Hare-Bowers who taught Afrikaans through the medium of Afrikaans not English, a challenge to many of the students.

The question of admission of men students

The admission of young men to TC was a matter that had already been aired and debated. Mr WA Stevens, the Principal of the Selbourne Primary School in East London and for a period a member of the Advisory Board of TC, raised this matter in the latter part of 1959. The question would have to be debated and voted on in the Community Chapter. Sister Truda feared that such a proposal would shock the Community profoundly! Dr Hobson, also a member of the Advisory Board, felt quite convinced that they should not take men students as it would alter the whole character of the place.

Mr Stevens was aware of the need for young men teachers in Primary Schools. He wanted young men to be given the background and opportunities that generations of young women had had at TC. In May 1960 Mr Stevens asked for permission to send the other members of the Board a memo on this subject. Later that year, canvassing opinion, Mr Stevens approached the Circuit Inspector who warmly approved of the idea. Mother Joanna Mary responded with a statement to the Members of the Board that such a proposal was not at all in line with their Mother Foundress's thought for the college and that they would need to submit any such proposal to the Community Chapter for careful consideration. There was the whole matter of residential accommodation to consider. Rhodes University was undergoing rapid expansion at that time and would not therefore consider the prospect of housing any TC male students.

Mr Stevens spoke to the Board on two occasions; the first in August 1959 and again in August 1960. He suggested that men students should be admitted not only to the third-year courses but to the general Primary Course. There was considerable discussion on this subject at the end of which Mr Stevens thanked the Chairman, the Revd Mother Superior and the Principal for the sympathetic consideration given to his views. That put the matter to rest for a time, but in 1964 Mr Stevens again raised the question of the admission of men students, as he wished them to enjoy the advantages of TC.

The Chairman of the Board, Dr SB Hobson, and Mr Slater were opposed to the whole idea of admitting men as they considered that it would jeopardise the good reputation the College enjoyed at that time. The Board Minutes for August note that the Inspectors had been unequivocally opposed to the suggestion of accepting male students at the College. The matter was laid to rest. There is no evidence that the proposal was ever put to the student body.

Problems with Rhodes men students

Relationships between the College and Rhodes men students were becoming problematic. On 6 May 1963 Sister Virginia wrote to Mr H M Roberts the Warden of Struben House: "Students of the University have been appropriating articles of underwear belonging to TC students and hung out on out-door lines to dry. The University students have been displaying these articles in the Common Room of Struben House. They regard the matter as a good joke (!!); but it seems to me that some of our young people have a very uneducated sense of what is in ordinary good taste and what is not..." Mr Roberts replied: "...apparently the culprits are not confined to Struben House, and the matter is being investigated at a higher level." This action by the Rhodes students was in bad taste but more was to follow.

In October the Principal wrote in stronger terms, this time to the Vice-Chancellor Dr Hyslop: "...we have at times had difficulty with men students from Rhodes, who visit our students at the College residences of an evening; and arrive rather the worse for drink. These men have on occasions made themselves very objectionable and have treated the House Sisters with scant respect when the latter have requested the men to leave... On one or two recent occasions, the young men have been so defiant and objectionable that I have advised the House Sisters to communicate at once with the Police... I should be glad to know whether you approve of the method I propose to employ?" The Vice-Chancellor replied "This kind of behaviour is something of which I strongly disapprove, and heavy penalties will be imposed upon the students found guilty..." The matter was left to the Rhodes authorities to handle.

There was further trouble some years later, this time involving riotous behaviour. Reported facts: "Shouting, stone-throwing, and the arrival of the police...two young men...one holding a bottle in his hand, came on to the Bangor stoep and tried to open the door, but on finding it locked, they left... On Thursday morning, 18 May, an empty champagne bottle found outside Beethoven..." These reports were sent to Rhodes and Sister Virginia received a note from Dr Rennie: "I am sorry that your staff have had to put up with this sort of thing; it really is disgraceful." Perhaps the Sisters were relieved that men students had not been admitted to TC!

National Union of South African Students

Relationships between NUSAS and the authorities at TC fluctuated between relative cordiality and criticism and hostility on both sides. In the late 1950s both Sister Madeline and Sister Truda in turn had agreed to be honorary vice-presidents of the movement. Sister Virginia however declined to accept the position when she was approached. Her correspondence with various of the NUSAS office-bearers became acrimonious on both sides.

She was not in sympathy with the movement and considered that NUSAS failed to appreciate the special position of TC. She pointed out in a letter that the College was founded and still owned and managed by a Religious Community on certain principles which they had not found it necessary to modify since the institution was founded.

The crux of her argument was that some years previously a representative of NUSAS forced the issue of 100% membership by the student body. She pointed out that from the early years of the College English-speaking and Dutch- (later Afrikaans-) speaking students were all made welcome. This had created a remarkable harmony throughout the 70 years of the College's existence. The only time she had ever known this harmony to be jeopardised was over the issue of NUSAS membership as the Afrikaans-speaking students refused to join. A real cleavage had resulted for a time and feelings ran high. The College authorities had no wish to run any such risk again.

Resignation of Sister Virginia

Sister Virginia had never enjoyed good health and the stresses and strains of office had worn her down. She submitted her resignation to the Manager in September 1969 thereby ending the line of Sisters Principal/Rector. The news was received with dismay by many people. Sister Virginia had been remarkable for her personal interest in the whole well-being of each of her girls. Her loving care had also produced a closely-knit staff and the happy atmosphere of the staff room was a good reflection of the spirit of the College.

An OG remembered that when Sister Virginia came through the door she exuded a quiet and calm dignity which did not depend on a loud voice. She knew all the students by name and they knew that she cared for them. Her quiet sense of humour was part of her personality. Another OG wrote: "No one messed with Sister Virginia! In those three short years under the watchful (one could say gimlet) eyes of Sister Virginia and her staff, we made the firmest friends, had more good times than bad and above all the spiritual dimension of our lives was awakened, nurtured and developed."

Apart from her ill health, Sister Virginia had other reasons for her decision. She was keenly aware of the fact that high qualifications were now required of lecturers in promotion posts, and that her own qualifications were below those required of heads of departments in training colleges. She felt it would be dishonest to continue to hold the post of Rector, and to retain a position of authority over experienced and competent lecturers who had been refused promotions to Head of Department because of a lack of the necessary qualification for that position.

There was also the strain of what in effect amounted to a dual existence. The work of administering the Training College had increased considerably. The day-to-day administration combined with the work of implementing the new three-year course and the prospect of an even heavier burden in the coming years when the principles of the new National Education Policy were implemented would impose a great strain on a Sister Rector, who together with her duties as head of the College had also to fulfil the obligations of the religious life.

On receipt of Sister Virginia's resignation, the Advisory Council explored all possible alternatives to the acceptance of the resignation. What was of importance to the Council was the close link with the Community which had given the College its distinctive character. Finally, it was resolved that the resignation of the Rector should be accepted.

It must be remembered that the Rector of TC was selected by the Manager, the Superior of the Community, and appointed by the Cape Education Department. Hence, the Rector was responsible to the Manager who in turn filled a double role as the representative authority of the Cape Administration and the Superior of the Community which owned TC and of which the Rector was a member. The Rector thus represented the ownership of the College in a way which no lay Rector appointed by a governing council could do and consequently the interests of the College were in a special way her own. It was probably with this in mind that Sister Truda had written many years previously to the Chief Inspector that the Community had always felt that if the College was to be administered by the Sisters they needed to have teaching Sisters and a Sister Principal. It would lose its distinctive character under a divided control.

Some years after her retirement from the Rectorship, Sister Virginia withdrew from the Community to nurse an ailing uncle. After his death she returned to the Community, was thereafter known as Sister Nonie and after a period in charge of the Retreat House at Hillandale was elected Mother Superior.

Significant changes anticipated

There were changes in the air, changes of a nature far more extensive than those happening internally at TC. In 1967 there were press reports of a proposal that training colleges should be greatly enlarged and become affiliated to universities. If such legislation were introduced, TC, as a privately owned but Government-aided College would be placed in a peculiar position. By the time of Sister Virginia's resignation, Parliament had passed the Teacher Training Bill. The writing was on the wall and so the manager had acted with intuitive practical sense when she expressed her hope that Mrs Enid Craig, then Vice-Rector, would continue in office beyond November 1969 although she would already have reached the age of 60, to retain an able and experienced person in the position. The Advisory Committee supported this suggestion unanimously. The future existence of TC was already in doubt.

Immediately it was made known that Mrs Craig had succeeded as Rector following the resignation of Sister Virginia, rumours began to spread that the Community had handed over the College. The Superior, Mother Mary Eleanor, issued a statement to the OGs: "What will happen in the future we do not know, but College still preserves its continuity as a 'Community College', despite changes in personnel, and there is still a very close bond between the Community and the College... Teacher training is at present in a state of flux. Many aspects are new and challenging. And only time will tell what the future holds for us in the way of new developments."

Where the training colleges were concerned it had become increasingly apparent that it was very difficult to get lady principals who were prepared to undertake the onerous task of heading up a combined scholastic and residential institution. Up to that time at TC the Sisters had undertaken it in their corporate strength and team-work. What was now to happen was in fact an act of faith and a step into the unknown.

CHAPTER 8

TC under Mrs Enid Craig and Miss Bridget Pilson
1970–1975

I N MRS CRAIG, TC had a worthy successor to Sister Virginia. She was conscious of the long tradition of TC and was determined to retain it. Writing to the OGs in 1971 she stressed that the work and the training continued as usual. The pattern stayed constant as did the aims and traditions of the College. Yet there were continual changes in small ways. New techniques and methods came in; rules changed or were adapted to fit the times, even the hem-lines at that time seemed uncertain and due for change! It was a difficult task to run a college with possibly only a few years of existence left. In March 1971 Mrs Craig discussed with a member of the Education Department the fact that it would be impossible, in the anomalous position in which the College was at that time, to advertise her post. It was agreed that the matter would be put before the Advisory Committee, a successor chosen from the existing staff, and a recommendation sent to the Department for approval.

At a meeting held on 13 August 1971 the Advisory Committee unanimously recommended Miss BA Pilson (then Vice-Rector) as the new Rector and in the event of the Department's approval of her appointment as Rector, the Advisory Committee recommended (again unanimously) that the choice of Vice-Rector fall on Mr JC Knox (HoD).

Before coming to TC Mrs Craig had been on the staff of the Uitenhage Training College. Miss Bridget Pilson was an OG of the College having been a student in 1939–1940, then a Lecturer 1943–1946, and 1963–1969, Vice-Rector 1970–1971, and finally Rector 1972–1975. When head-hunted by Sister Truda in 1962 Miss Pilson had written: "TC has always turned out good teachers and it would be nice to feel that in a small way I had contributed towards shaping that final product. I have not forgotten the start TC gave to my teaching career. I have always felt deeply indebted to the College." Miss Pilson held office until closure in 1975.

An OG (1970–1972) remembered that Miss Pilson walked briskly, talked in well-enunciated but clipped tones and was strict but utterly fair in decision making. In a note to Miss Christina Wiseman who had applied for the position of Lady Warden, Miss Pilson mentioned: "Our girls are a lively lot, but way-out dress and hairstyles are frowned upon and you should not find too much of the permissive trend has crept in here, though they naturally have more freedom than students of the past."

The Community was no longer able to provide Sisters to run the boarding hostels, so lay staff were appointed. The new regime of hostel staff aimed to uphold the principles by which the hostels had been run by the Sisters. They met to discuss and consider amendments to rules sought by the students. The Lady Warden of Lincoln reported that as 1973 would be the last year College would be operating fully with four hostels, they were unwilling to jeopardise the good name of the College at the last lap. "Coming back into hostels with boyfriends after the cinema – No!"

In 1970 up-to-date dress rules were issued for all students as follows: For lectures, tests, and examinations: neat frocks, reasonable length; shoes or sandals (not beach sandals); no short socks (except with gym uniform or tennis frocks); hair – loose if collar length, if longer, tied back neatly or done up; bobby sox may be worn. For teaching: frocks, not more than 4ins from the ground when kneeling; shoes and stockings; hair neatly tied back. For leisure wear: slacks may be worn – on College campus or Rhodes campus; in the Botanical gardens; on excursions out-of-town; in Beaufort Street and Beaufort Street cafés only; NOT in any other street at any time; slax-suits, but no other form of slacks may be worn out; culottes, if well cut and reasonable may be worn.

College authorities were always conscious of the need for guidance and training of student teachers concerning dress, in the important aspect of developing the personality, appearance, and bearing, so essential to successful teaching. Sister Virginia had summed up the changed approach in this way: "If we are to be true to Mother Cecile's vision and her spirit, we must make sure, so far as we possibly can, that we approach the modern student in modern terms. We are convinced that it is possible to do this without sacrificing anything of the fundamental principles upon which Mother Cecile founded the College 73 years ago." Every effort was made to meet the modern 17–21-year-old girl where she was, and this necessarily involved some radical adaptation in their methods of approach.

Music School post-1963

Sister Virginia had written to the Departmental Organiser of Music in April 1963 that TC no longer had a Music School covering all aspects of music training. The emphasis was then on Class Music and Class Singing. The College was also aware that schools needed teachers who were able to play the piano. The aim of the staff at that time was to ensure that as many students as possible had the ability to conduct Class Singing lessons well and play the piano if necessary. Some would only be able to play the guitar or recorder.

Addressing the music staff during her time as Rector, Mrs Craig recalled that this had once been a Music School in the real sense of the word in that it trained real musicians but when the Rhodes University Music Department introduced the B. Mus. degree the College School of Music had declined. What she went on to say must have been hurtful to some, but it summed up the situation. She felt that the aura of the past was perhaps blinding them to their present function. They had to adapt to the fact that at that point the Music Department existed as a part of the total training set-up in which they were all engaged. Its main function was not to train pianists as such but to assist and supplement the Class Music course.

The piano work was important and involved the music staff in considerable hard work often at an unrewarding level, but it counted for little in actual marks. In a limited way music was still alive and kicking at TC. Mr Bilsbury joined the staff in 1969 and formed a choir of about 50 students on a voluntary basis. This was termed the College Choir and it gave a number of public performances as well as being invited to sing as guest artists for three consecutive years at the East London Schools' Music Festival. The choir also recorded a programme for the SABC. The enthusiasm and interest exuded by Mr Bilsbury encouraged the members of the choir to give of their best and under his expert direction and training it rendered polished performances. His enthusiasm and interest also resulted in increasing numbers of students taking Class Music as a subject.

The charm of the St Peter's Campus

The Training College was, and now Rhodes University is, fortunate not only in possessing the fine buildings of the St Peter's campus for which

Mother Cecile had worked so hard but also in the natural beauty of the surroundings. An OG recalls the shaded beauty of the park-like grounds, the shrubs, the flowers, the trees, the well-kept lawns and Sister Lillian Frances tending with pride and love the seedlings coming to life. In *The Vocal Discord* in November 1970, a student newspaper of the last years of the existence of TC, one of the students wrote of the meaning of these buildings to the students. This article was later reprinted in the College Magazine. "Solid and serene with the mellowness of maturity, they form an integral part of the environment which created them, being ivy-speckled and earth coloured with the stamp of the soil from which they sprang. They breathe peace and the quiet satisfaction of fulfilment. To the traditionalists the old is infinitely more attractive than the new. To TC students the old is unforgettable. Who can speak of TC without imagining its red brick buildings on which one can see the slow turning of green to gold as the ivy leaf progresses through the seasons; the unique hostels with their cube rooms containing those Flapper-Age jugs and basins and those two-dimensional baths; the gold-fish pond reflecting slices of blue as the sky juts through among the myriad oak leaves rustling overhead; the Chapel with its squeaky kneelers, and its pink and blue fresco; the dark wood panelling in the dining room and the creaking back doors that usually have to be held closed with a table mat."

The Inspectors wrote of the picturesque setting of the College, the Chapel at its centre and the School of Music as an integral part, all of which reinforced the efforts of the staff to train teachers with the widest possible professional and cultural interests. In her time as Principal, Sister Frances Mary had mulled over the campus and the wonderful heritage it represented. She considered how much anxious thought must have gone into it all as the various buildings rose for growing needs and how much more thought and anxiety went into the paying for them! She was pondering ways and means for the worthy completion of the College approximately as designed in 1908. Mother Cecile was to wear herself out pleading for money for what she considered a righteous cause. She considered teacher training important enough to go on begging for money even after she had become extremely ill. Rhodes University entered into a fine heritage when purchasing this gracious addition to the University campus.

CHAPTER **9**

The lead-up to the closure of the College

SISTER FRANCES MARY wrote in the College Log Book on 11 May 1932: "Saw *Cape Times* account of Dr Malan's Speech at Huguenot University College, stating inevitability of Government taking over Training Colleges in very near future." On 27 May 1932 the Secretary General of Education paid a half-hour visit to TC. There had been private discussion concerning Government control. They were reassured that nothing would happen immediately, and that TC would receive special treatment in the arrangement of particulars. This was not elucidated further. As early as 1918 Sister Clare had mentioned in a Quarterly Report that universities were offering T2 courses. Those were courses for the upper end of the Primary School. Students could combine a teacher training course with some academic subjects leading to the B.A. degree.

This was not entirely in line with the training college approach. Sister Clare felt this was an inevitable development that was likely to benefit education in the long run. What was certain was that it would draw off students from colleges and so reduce numbers for the ordinary T2 course. Further she felt it would not be of much benefit to education unless the training part of the work was made more thorough and practical than it had been.

In 1929 Sister Kate reported that the opinion abroad as well as in South Africa was divided as to the wisdom of making Primary training a concern of the universities. The authorities at the training colleges fully believed in their competence to deal with Primary teacher training and did not wish to undertake Secondary training which was appropriate to the University. A strong consensus in favour of university training for teachers emerged from the Education Conference held in Pretoria in July 1928.

At an important conference held in Cape Town in January 1929, University Institutions and the training of teachers was discussed. The report following this conference stated that the training of teachers should be recognised as a function of the universities. It was held to be of the greatest importance to education generally that teachers should have the benefit of a university training and the wider and more scientific outlook which it implied. The universities were the proper training grounds for the professions and it was an anomalous situation that the profession of teaching should to a large extent still be excluded from the advantages which a university training could offer.

It was the trend in other countries that training for the profession of teaching was made the concern of universities. This was clearly in conflict with what the Cape Education Department desired to achieve. The comment that followed on this in the Gazette challenged the statement that universities were the proper training grounds because it suggested more than the facts warranted.

The benefits of special training colleges

The Cape Education Department was strongly in favour of the training of secondary school teachers being the responsibility of universities while the training of primary school teachers should be a matter for special training colleges. This approach was important. If the newly trained primary teachers were to be capable of responsible teaching work from the beginning of their service (which was what was required of them) then the two-year course had to be an intensive professional course as offered in the training colleges.

The training of primary school teachers involved a great deal of detailed instruction in methods. This was alien to the true function of a university and would be inefficiently carried out at such institutions. Whatever efforts were made by the legislators, officials and inspectors for the advancement of education, in the final issue the matter rested with the teacher; and one of the most valuable treasures a country could possess was a body of well-qualified teachers.

Sister Frances Mary speaking from the standpoint of the training college raised the same issue at the Queenstown Teachers' Conference in June 1932. She spoke of an academic education versus professional training. There was the University model of knowledge for its own sake or the Training College model which put the child in the centre. The Primary teacher's training in her opinion was good but it was different to university training.

It was important to remember that the student had not opted for primary teaching because he/she lacked the brains or the money. It was largely a matter of temperament and taste. The closeness to human nature, to childhood and to service where the need was so obvious and the response so undisguised, made its own special appeal to some natures and probably to women rather than to men. In the two-year course at Training Colleges she felt that the academic preparation in the first instance should be left to the High Schools and that any further study of special subjects should be mainly devoted to the best methods of presenting them in the Primary School. She wondered if those who criticised training college standards realised what a student grappled with in such an array – often reaching a fine standard too. She thought there ought to be a *via media* between such generalisation (i.e. training college curriculum) and university specialisation.

Dr Malherbe's stance

Dr EG Malherbe, the eminent educationalist, attended the same conference as a guest speaker. In the Principal's report on the conference to the Advisory Board she mentioned that Dr Malherbe made an unequivocal statement of his case for the university control of all teacher training; though he publicly repeated a remark which he had just made to her in private that it was neither his desire nor intention to abolish TC which he considered made a unique contribution to teacher training.

The 1934 Educational Conference was described by Dr Malherbe as the largest and most comprehensive conference on education ever held in South Africa. The training of primary school teachers was discussed. The general opinion appeared to favour universities.

Dr DF Malan, Minister of Education at that time, instructed Dr Malherbe to make a survey of the whole teacher training situation. The results showed that primary teachers trained at universities eventually held higher positions than those trained in training colleges. Publication of these results sparked off a big controversy between the Secretary for Education and the four Provincial Directors of Education. This controversy turned up like a recurring decimal over the subsequent fifty years and became the subject of several government commissions. In the *Proceedings of the*

National Conference on English-speaking South Africa which reported on the conference held in July 1974, it was clearly stated that it was only "ideological jealousies on the part of the provinces that prevented all (teacher) training coming under the aegis of the universities".

Relations between TC and the Education Department

It had been the wish of Mother Cecile, the Founder always to work in harmony with the Education Authorities stemming from the fine relationship both she and Sister Clare had had with Dr Muir, the Inspectors, and indeed the whole Department. The Department had always shown respect and consideration towards the aims and ideals of TC but under the Nationalist Government (post 1948) times were changing.

Just before she relinquished her position as Principal, Sister Truda placed on record that "our personal contacts with chief inspectors are excellent and friendly. In these personal contacts one tends to forget or discount the distant rumble from parliamentary debates on a National Education Advisory Council which gives autocratic control into the hands of the Minister of Education." She wondered what Mother Cecile would have said. Undoubtedly the Mother would have urged – "... Go on doing what we are trying to do – to work with them, as long as they wish to work with us; to give generously and pray unceasingly." The SGE at the time, Mr Liebenberg, had the highest regard for Sister Truda personally as Principal and for TC which he regarded as one of the best training colleges in the country.

To the relief of the Community the working relations with the SGE and with the Chief Inspector of the Cape Education Department continued to be most cordial.

Political uncertainty

Several of the Sisters had expressed apprehension as to whether these friendly relations would continue under the government of the day and there were grounds for apprehension in that the SGE was under the direction of the Administrator of the Cape Province, a political appointee. The Chapter Minutes of the Community commented on the uncertain situation of having a government party in power with which they did not feel much sympathy and from whom they feared unwelcome interference.

The SGE had written in 1966 that Education could never remain static because it was closely related to the needs of society. It was important for education policy to keep pace with the latest developments. The Principal in her report for November 1967 wondered if members of the Board had noticed reports in the press of a proposal that training colleges should be greatly enlarged and become affiliated to universities. This had first been mentioned about two years previously. In which case TC would be placed in a peculiar position if legislation were introduced to affiliate colleges with universities.

Training College in Port Elizabeth: A threat?

During the 1940s, especially during the War, there had been fewer students at TC. Fortunately, at that time and for the next fifteen years TC became the official Training College of the Rhodesian and Federal Education Departments. After the revision of salary scales in the mid-1950s when primary school teachers were placed on the same scale as secondary teachers, enrolment picked up. The threat of a training college in Port Elizabeth hung over TC and the Community like the sword of Damocles. In Departmental circles it was hoped that the establishment of a parallel-medium college for men and women in Port Elizabeth would be of great benefit to education in the Eastern Province.

In 1955 the Principal had mentioned to the Advisory Board that the opinion in Port Elizabeth was that the establishment of a Training College there would encourage enrolment of male student teachers. At the time Departmental policy was to improve and enlarge existing colleges as was happening in Britain and the USA. For years there was uncertainty about the proposed College for Port Elizabeth. The Department appeared anxious to protect TC against the opening of a training college in Port Elizabeth and so urged TC to continue with a maximum enrolment. If this was not done, then the Department would inevitably have to open another college. Kimberley was suggested as a possible location, but Port Elizabeth had been promised the College. But enrolments to English-speaking colleges were fluctuating from year to year. The College authorities found themselves on the horns of a dilemma. Was a college in Port Elizabeth a threat or an opportunity to re-vamp the campus with fewer students?

Once again, the College was in dire straits. Sister Virginia wrote the Editorial for the Magazine on this matter: "We have reached the stage now where our revenue does not even cover current expenditure, despite our efforts to economise. There is no reserve fund – all loans taken out are 'permanent' loans – we continue to pay interest without redeeming capital." The answer lay in a drastic increase in fees. If TC was to be able to offer amenities comparable with those of Departmental colleges, and at the same time maintain its own special character, which made it unique, there was simply no option but to increase fees. And while that something special could not be assessed in rands and cents, it was nevertheless worth paying for.

Possibility of a National System of Education

The SGE Report for 1968 made it clear that where teacher training was concerned the policy of the Department was henceforth to be a national system and that draft legislation was to be brought before Parliament. Owing to the divergent views expressed, particularly on the future role of the Provinces in the training of primary school teachers, the Bill was withdrawn and the matter was referred to a select Committee. The Minutes of the Advisory Board reveal that at the Meeting on 10 November 1967 Dr James Hyslop referred to the uncertainty of the future of TC. It was clear that the College would be affected by the new Education Bill which was yet to be published. This is the first reference in the archives to the possible closure of the College as it was at that time administered. This was a matter that was to bedevil the College authorities for several years, a situation made more difficult by the prevarication of the Department.

Attempts by the Manager to get clarification went unanswered. Even after the decision to close was taken there was still a degree of stalling as no answer was forthcoming as to when the last intake should be admitted. At the meeting of the Advisory Board in November 1967 the Principal had pointed to yet another dilemma. Until the findings of the Commission were made known the future was uncertain. The Advisory Board was unable to contemplate embarking on any major building project without the assurance that a new hostel would be required for a reasonable number of years thereafter. It is important not to underestimate the uncertainty that surrounded the Bill and what it entailed for the future of the College.

Lack of consultation

There were certain factors that the authorities at TC found alarming. Enormous and arbitrary powers were to be placed in the hands of the Minister of Education. The whole concept was being imposed from the top and those who were engaged in the work of preparing primary teachers were never consulted. The proposed Institutes of Education were a nebulous concept. Furthermore, little indication had been given of what was envisaged for future teacher training or how that training was to be implemented.

At the time it was difficult to foresee what the implications were, first, for teacher training and education in general; secondly, for the training colleges and particularly TC which was in a unique position, being privately owned; or thirdly, for the personnel of TC whose future and livelihood would undoubtedly be affected. The project properly handled certainly held much promise. It could usher in a new and even splendid era in Teacher Training. The system of large Institutes of Education already worked well overseas. But while there was ignorance over what was envisaged it was impossible even to begin assessing the impact of the Bill on already existing institutions.

Uncertainty over the future

In a letter written in May 1968 the Acting Principal Mrs Craig expressed the feeling at the time: "... We are all feeling anxious – naturally – and apprehensive about the Bill. One cannot be so reactionary as to set one's face against all change, and...condemn it out of hand. But our College... has a long and proud tradition of service; and we should be sad indeed to have to watch it lose its character and identity unless we were very sure it would be for the better."

The Principal Sister Virginia submitted a memorandum to the Select Committee and appeared before the Committee to offer oral evidence. She pointed out that TC was one of the pioneers in teacher training. She described the College as a "deeply religious foundation" and stressed that it had a "long and proud tradition of service". Concerning the pattern of training envisaged in the proposed legislation she argued that it would affect the character of the College. At TC the emphasis had always been on the training in sound Christian principles as well as a sound professional training. "In our view it should be a great loss to education in general and particularly to teacher training, if this aspect of our training were discarded or if some other form of religious influence were substituted for this well-tried and effective pattern."

What should not be overlooked was the fact that the training colleges had built up over the years a fund of accumulated knowledge, skill and experience in teacher training, and more importantly, had trained and experienced personnel. The College authorities were anxious that the proposed institutes for the training of teachers should make full use of what was of value and readily available in the experience and personnel of the existing colleges. At the same time, it was stressed that the universities had little experience in or few trained personnel for the training of teachers for primary school posts.

The TC staff considered that the only effective teacher training in the Cape Province at that time was done by the training colleges. To destroy this in favour of university-based and -controlled teaching would be disastrous; the university courses envisaged for all primary teachers would eliminate half the TC students who were not academically capable of coping with them. Where then would they get the required numbers of teachers to staff the schools?

There was great apprehension at the uniform slant likely to be imposed on all institutions and provinces with too much being decided by those at the top. The approach was seen by the staff as being dictatorial with no consultation with those engaged in the actual work. So much here has an almost prophetic note about it. The training colleges of the Cape Province had a long and proud tradition of service; they had for more than 50 years turned out competent teachers.

Following on the report submitted by the Select Committee, Parliament amended the National Education Policy Act (Act No 39 of 1967). The Legislation was subsequently approved as the National Education Amendment Act (No 73 of 1969). Two points to notice were first, the Minister of National Education was empowered to determine the policy to be followed with regard to the training of teachers. Secondly, the training of teachers for primary and pre-primary schools was to be provided at a college under the control of the State (including Provincial Administration) or a university. This was to come into effect from a date determined by the Minister and such training was to be provided at a college and a university working in close collaboration. The nub of the matter was "at a date to be decided". Where did TC come in all this? Was TC to be incorporated into or affiliated with Rhodes University?

The writing was on the wall – purchase by Rhodes?

Grahamstown was too small a centre to carry any more student teachers than those already enrolled at TC and the University. Even then TC used all the Government schools in Grahamstown for practice teaching purposes to the maximum of their ability to provide classes. Fortunately, the private schools in Grahamstown graciously co-operated and so made it possible for all the students to be provided with practice teaching.

An Extraordinary Meeting of the Community Chapter was called for Wednesday 11 September 1970 for the Sisters to vote upon the proposed amalgamation of the Training College with Rhodes University. The Superior reported on all that had happened since the introduction of the Parliamentary Bill. Clearly the writing was on the wall where TC was concerned, and the College authorities were alert enough to begin making plans.

Dr Hyslop wrote to the Minister of Education concerning the future of the University and the Training College and "received a non-committal though not discouraging reply". On 6 May 1970 the Director wrote to the Superior stating that the Department was not prepared to take over TC. The reason was that "Grahamstown is too small a centre to allow for sufficient expansion and the Department has committed itself to the establishment of a Training College in Port Elizabeth to which it is giving its support." It was made clear that the Department was not prepared to continue to subsidise TC indefinitely; it was not prepared to set a date, nor did it want to close the College, but they believed that numbers at TC would shrink when the Port Elizabeth college was established to such an extent that this College would no longer be an economic proposition. The TC authorities were advised to approach Rhodes as to the possibility of an amalgamation with their Education Faculty.

The Superior and Mrs Craig then had a meeting with Dr Hyslop and the Professors of Education, Morton and Gerber. Dr Hyslop indicated that the University was interested in the College properties to the north of the Port Elizabeth road; i.e. the main College block, the Memorial Hall, hostels and Beethoven House, the intention being to make these the headquarters of the Education faculty. At that time Rhodes was not interested in the Chapel or in the buildings occupied by the Sisters beyond the Kowie Ditch. At that point in the discussions it was thought that Rhodes would take over the first-year enrolment from 1972 taking three years to absorb and finally take over the whole enrolment. The process was seen to be "absorption" rather than "amalgamation".

Position of TC staff?

Regarding TC staff the Superior indicated that Professor Gerber, who gave the impression that the Director had discussed the matter fully with him, gave the assurance that the Cape Education Department would protect the TC staff with regard to salaries, leave privileges, etc. Dr Hyslop indicated that some of the staff could become part of Rhodes, but the question of staff was not considered in detail. Dr Hyslop undertook to interview the Director and the Minister of Education concerning finance. He wished to know from the Community which properties they were prepared to sell to the University and at what price.

The Community Trustees met on Tuesday 1 September 1970 to discuss these proposals and passed the following resolution: "...that, should the negotiations now proceeding be successful, and a price and terms acceptable to the Trustees be offered, the Trustees approve in principle of the sale to Rhodes University of the land and buildings comprising the educational and boarding establishment of the Training College, or of so much thereof as may be required."

Could TC not be saved?

There were certain matters that had to be considered some of which were non-negotiable. The Community would under no circumstances be able to finance the College without departmental grants. An enormous amount of capital would be required to meet teachers' salaries, maintenance costs and general running expenses, capital which the Community did not possess. The decline in the number of Sisters in the Community meant that there were no Sisters available to staff the College. Mrs Craig was already on pension and had made it clear that she would not be available to continue as Rector after 1971. The Superior noted that it was extremely difficult to find women principals but that even if they could be sure of having suitable lay staff it would be difficult to continue to run the College as a Community College.

When Mrs Craig had been appointed Rector, because there was no Sister to assume the position, the Community was led to wonder just how much influence they still had in the College. Finance was not available to support what would then have become a private institution. Miss Pilson the next Rector had only one teaching Sister on her staff and, apart from the fact that the Superior was the Manager, the Community had little to do with the day-to-day administration of the College. The Sisters were no longer running the boarding side of the College. Furthermore, for certificates to be recognised as valid they had to be issued either by a university or by the Education Department. Certificates issued by a private college would be valueless. The moment had to be seized and Rhodes was willing to purchase the College.

Rhodes University was planning considerable expansion and development over the following ten years. The fact that they were willing to negotiate and absorb the TC campus as part of their plans for the development of the Rhodes campus came at an opportune time for the Training College and the Community. If they delayed, the opportunity might be lost as East London was pressing the university to encourage and support the founding of a training college in that city.

Closure – Community decision

So the Community, as the Mother Superior put it, took the decision to "bring to an honourable end, and with our reputation unimpaired, our College which has served the cause of education in this country, and whose influence will continue for many generations to come, being thankful to God for the way in which He has blessed and prospered this work through the years, and being grateful that He has provided this opportunity for us to be absorbed into a liberal university which will be concerned to uphold the traditions of our College and that the buildings into which so much love and labour has been poured, will still be used in the service of education in this country."

The Resolution proposed by Sister Virginia at the Chapter Meeting on 11 September 1970 and seconded by Sister Margery read: "That this Community signifies its consent to the absorption of the Grahamstown Teacher Training College into Rhodes University: this absorption of College to be accomplished in such stages and on such terms as may be agreed upon by the authorities of the College and of the University respectively." The members of the Community voted in favour of the motion. Thus, the Sisters themselves took the decision to bring the life of the College to a definitive close and did not have the decision made for them. These proceedings were to remain strictly confidential for the time being.

It remained a stressful situation. The Superior concluded the Special Chapter Meeting with the words: "Our Mother Foundress would, I am sure, be with us in this matter. She founded the College from scratch, from nothing. Now she would surely say to us, go forward with courage. This is another step on the way!" The matter of confidentiality was again stressed by the Superior at a Chapter Meeting in June 1970: "This matter is still in a highly confidential and tentative state and we must be very careful not to mention anything outside. There are sure to be rumours, but all we can say, if asked, is that nothing has yet been decided about the future of TC."

Where to next?

Matters continued to move slowly. There had been meetings and consultations between the College Trustees and the Rhodes authorities and Dr Hyslop had drawn up a memorandum which he intended to present in person to the Director of Education and the Administrator in January 1971. What was urgently needed was Departmental approval as soon as possible of the scheme for the absorption of TC into Rhodes University. Dr Hyslop presented his memorandum and Dr Malan, the Administrator of the Cape, gave the nod and hoped that this would result in an increased number of English-Medium teachers of whom there was an alarming shortage.

Part of the urgency was that students for 1972 would submit their applications as early as February 1971; also, the staff would need to be put in the picture as soon as possible. The College Trustees had presented a figure which was to be the basis for negotiations for the purchase of the College buildings. The Superior felt that the Sisters should give some thought to what the Community should do with the money received. It was important to bear in mind that the funds for many of the buildings had been raised by gifts, donations and public subscriptions for a specific purpose. The Community could not keep the money for themselves apart from that needed for the construction of their new home in Donkin Street. It was agreed that much of it ought to go back into the Church and be used for Education.

Rumours multiplied until eventually in April 1971 the Rector asked Dr Hyslop for permission to break the seal of confidentiality to inform the staff and students. In the archives there is a five-page hand-written letter by Mrs Craig used for this purpose. She introduced the topic by referring to the rumours circulating about the future of the College. They were true. She went on to offer explanation and clarification. The Rector outlined the position much as the Superior had to the Chapter with this addition: "With regard to staff... and College employees. I cannot guarantee anything where the College staff is concerned. I do not know whether any of you will be employed by Rhodes or would wish to be. Certainly, the College will need to be manned and run until the end of 1974 for our students. And almost certainly Rhodes will require personnel for the hostel, kitchen and grounds, etc. More than that, I cannot at this stage tell you."

This was a most unsatisfactory position in which to leave the staff. She concluded with an appeal: "If you can, without jeopardising your own careers and interests, give us as long service as possible, we shall be grateful. If you must, in your own interests, take a job elsewhere before the end of 1974, naturally we could not expect you to forego it and would not raise any demur. But if and when staff leave, we are going to find it extremely difficult to replace them in the circumstances."

Mrs Craig gave much the same report to the students with the assurance, "I want to reassure all of you, and your parents who may be hearing these rumours, and be alarmed, that all of you at present in the College, and at least all next year's first years, will complete your training as departmental students on present lines, at this College. There will be no question of your having to transfer to another College, nor of an interruption in your course. And 1972 first-years will enrol here as usual."

Options?

Mrs Craig described the whole episode as a staggering and sad development. There was little option in the matter, but the decision taken had been preceded by much thought, discussion and prayer. The Department was not prepared to buy the College and take it over because it was too small to fit into the new scheme of training which involved large colleges of possibly 1000 students. The Community was no longer able to provide the personnel to staff the College either as teaching Sisters or as Hostel staff. If the Department cut off the financial aid the life of the College would end. It was better to close while the College was still alive and vital and well-respected. It was finally agreed that the last intake would be in 1973 and that the College would close at the end of 1975. The irony of the situation was that applications were still being received by TC in good numbers even though closure was imminent. Rhodes would gradually acquire some of the property from the beginning of 1974.

Mrs Craig concluded, "I know this all comes as a tremendous blow to all of you – it does to all of us." It was a sad end to a College whose reputation extended far and wide; a College with a wealth of tradition. There was no other option than to close. "Believe me", added Mrs Craig, "we have explored every possible alternative. And always we come back to the realisation that without departmental financial support we are helpless. And that support will come to an end; it is only a matter of time. The interim period during change-over will be full of problems of readjustment. We shall do all we can to keep things normal as long as possible; and hope to keep our flag flying and our standards high until the end. We shall need your prayers and good wishes. I am quite sure we shall have them." At no point was the Community asked to close the College; but the Department did state that they could not guarantee that the College could continue as a state-aided institution indefinitely.

And so, after 81 years, the College closed its doors at the end of 1975. In the Annual Report of the Director of Education the only reference to this closure is: "There was a decrease of one Teachers' College as a result of the closing of the Teachers' College at Grahamstown." The Director of Education was unable to attend the final Founder's Day/Reunion but sent a letter which was read out on the occasion. It expressed his thanks for the part played by the College in providing teachers of high standing.

10

The Diaspora

I N THE TC Magazine in March 1914 the spread of the OGs is described in this way: "Some seventy students of last year have now entered upon their work of teaching and are scattered up and down the land from far away Taungs in the northern desert to green Port Alfred on the southern sea; and from Willowdale in the eastern territories to Touws River and Caledon in the distant west."

When Mother Cecile started the Training School in 1884 teaching was not an attractive occupation in the Cape Colony. The wide-open spaces and the freedom of the veld held greater appeal. Mother Cecile had toured for weeks to find girls for the first classes for teacher training at St Peter's School. She achieved her objective and some of the Dutch girls came from more than a thousand miles away to be trained. By 1904, 300 young women trained at St Peter's had already been sent out to teach in the Government schools of South Africa.

Mother Cecile writing in 1904 mentioned over 300 teachers trained in Grahamstown who were then employed as teachers and who had proved their efficiency and goodness. There had been 94 students in the Training School the previous December and there were 64 waiting for admission. By the time that Sister Clare retired in 1920 the College Magazine recorded that over 2000 students had passed through College under Sister Clare and had experienced her stimulating personality and guidance. Sister Clare had emphasised the lessons of truthfulness, thoroughness, practical patriotism, grit – lessons often recalled with fuller meaning as life went on. All students were entered for the examination when the time came. Between 1894 and 1904, 519 students were entered for the examination. Of these, 486 passed with 212 of them in the First Grade. This was a remarkable achievement. It was also confidently assumed that most would teach initially for two or three years before being married, but it was also hoped that they would not be lost entirely to the teaching profession even thereafter.

Margaret Furse the Secretary to the EHU wrote in 1903 to the members of the Union that almost always the students were wanted for different schools before their training term was over. Many of them went out to distant and lonely places where they often did fine work as missionaries as well as their secular teaching. Students were drawn from a wide area. By 1916 there were three from Rhodesia, several from the Free State and Griqualand East and other distant places. Younger sisters and cousins tended to follow in the steps of their elders.

Influence of TC

When Dr Muir addressed the students in August 1909 he told them that he saw the good influence of TC at work in other parts of the country. He had recently toured the Transkei and East Griqualand for a month and had found Grahamstown girls in many places. On the second day after he had left Butterworth he had visited a school that used to be rather notorious in the Education Office; but instead of the old male teacher, he had found a TC teacher, Miss Barr. He said that it had been a pleasure to see the difference in that school; there was good order and neatness, the children were bright and keen. As an educationalist he had found it a cheering experience.

Judge President Kotze spoke of his own experiences travelling around his circuit. The opinion of outsiders was that TC was doing excellent work. This was the result of his own observation and experience. Not merely did the number of the students testify to the good work of the institution, but wherever he went in his Circuits through the Colony and the Territories, even in remote Kokstad and Natal, he heard its praises sung.

Sister Mary Noel who was for a time on the staff of TC mentioned that wherever she went in the Eastern Cape raising money for the Orphanage, she either met an OG or heard news of them. She said that this gave her the pleasant feeling of being at home everywhere. It also made her aware of the responsibility on the part of the College in sending out so many students each year to all parts of South Africa. She pointed out that the responsibility also rested on those who went out so full of courage year by year to do their work.

Bishop Michael Furse (Bishop of Pretoria 1909–1920) reported that in travelling about the country, wherever he found a TC-trained teacher he noticed something about the school and the girl and the tone of the place that he did not find anywhere else.

In her speech at the final Founder's Day in 1975 the Mother Superior, Mary Eleanor, spoke of all the students who had passed through the doors of the College and gone out to be educators, not only in South Africa, but almost all over the world – Japan, Australia, New Zealand, USA, Canada, Alaska, Great Britain, Kenya, Malawi, Zambia, Rhodesia, Indonesia, South West Africa and Greece (various Sisters had received letters from OGs in each of these places). Each took with them the indelible mark of the traditions and devotion which had made TC what it was.

So from that growing cluster of buildings a constant stream of trained teachers went out into the world. It was not easy for an 18-year-old far from home to face a world of strangers, bravely and gently and lovingly learning the precious, painful lessons that only experience can teach, that only love and humility can truly learn. Some made a sad mess of it, but none can help being young and inexperienced when making a start in life.

Lily Ferguson whose home was in Kimberley was teaching at the school in Richmond. She described how at the start of term when she was faced with the problem of teaching through the medium of Afrikaans she had felt like giving up. There were eleven teachers on the staff of whom she was the only English-speaker. She admitted that she was picking up Dutch quite nicely from hearing it constantly spoken.

The Cape Education Gazette for November 1904, quoting from an article entitled "Openings for Women Teachers in South Africa" endorsed the following: "The teacher in South Africa is not looked upon as an intellectual machine but takes a very important part in the social life of the country. For this reason, much is demanded of her, not merely regarding her work from a technical point of view, but as regards her influence on a large social circle. She must be adaptable, sympathetic, wide in her interests, able to respond to demands for help in ways of which she has had no experience. The teacher is expected to bring to her work an added grace and dignity." The young teachers going out from the College must have felt much as Daniel did when faced with the lions in their den!

Bishop Cornish (Bishop of Grahamstown 1899–1915) expressed his opinion that the influence of those going out to teach would be far greater than that of the politicians in Cape Town because they would have to deal with the rising generation which was impressionable and receptive. They would have opportunities which politicians would never have for doing good. Teachers trained at TC went to all parts of the Colony carrying with them the spirit and enthusiasm imparted to them by those responsible for their training.

Sir Thomas Graham speaking in 1939 recalled that Mother Cecile had laid down high standards and he believed that the standard of teaching at TC was higher than in any other institution in the Union. He considered that College-trained teachers were the elite of the profession in the Union.

In the training of young women as teachers the Sisters had set themselves an ideal for which to aim: first, to train Christian women of high principle and character, who would go out to do God's work in the schools to which they were sent. Secondly, they were to be fully, adequately and well equipped for the work they had to do. And thirdly, these trained women should then spread their influence, where possible, into the homes of the children they taught.

Bishop Vyvian, a former Bishop of Zululand and after his retirement Warden to the Sisters, wrote to the EHU that the influence of TC on the students, and their influence in turn on the schools where they taught, spread over the whole country. It was recognised that there were many Christian homes which owed their standards in life to the tone of the College.

The Revd H B Ellison, another Warden to the Community in Grahamstown, speaking at the Annual Meeting of the EHU in 1911 said of TC-trained teachers that "...unconsciously they were doing more good... than the whole bench of bishops in South Africa..." The Bishops were probably not too happy about this reflection on their effectiveness.

Miss EB Hawkins, Headmistress of Wynberg Girls' High School and former Inspectress of Religious Instruction, spoke of her own experiences in this regard. "Few educational institutions leave a mark on their students as unmistakeable as the mark left on students of differing races and languages and temperaments and backgrounds by their two to three years here... I have moved about the country in the course of my professional life of just forty years. I have nearly always been able very quickly to recognise old TC girls among the teachers with whom I have come into contact." She singled out particularly their sense of dedication towards their professional work, the genuine concern for the things of the mind and the spirit, and a willingness to experiment. These were the things at work in the schools to which the OGs were appointed.

Many of the young women trained in Grahamstown had to go to lonely parts of the country. Here they not only had to teach but also faced the task of moulding the character of South African children. In this respect the holistic training they had received was important. They did their work well and enjoyed a high reputation with the educational authorities. The College had given them a broad outlook, and this was reflected in their teaching.

At TC the students received a liberal education. There was a deliberate attempt by the Sisters and teachers to encourage open discussion and enquiry; different viewpoints were tolerated (and not only in matters of religion); it was hoped to foster critical and questioning minds. The students were helped to see each person as an individual and not as someone of a particular racial category or language group. The School/College was composed of girls of different religious affiliations, of English or Dutch families, from wealthy or poor backgrounds.

At the final Founder's Day Mother Mary Eleanor referred to the hundreds of students who had gone out from the College and who had touched and influenced the lives of hundreds of children, who in their turn had influenced others. She saw the process as enduring because it relied on the characters and integrity of truly devoted women.

Sister Millicent wrote that when one was working at TC it seemed a comparatively small piece of work but that if one travelled about SA one found that it was a big thing. Everywhere, in large towns, in small *dorps,* at railway stations and on lonely farms, one saw the familiar hat-band or the OG badge.

The farm school and the One-Teacher School

The Cape Province and indeed much of southern Africa was sparsely populated. A member of staff at TC wrote to the EHU of the nature of the work in a remote area. She outlined that for instance in the Cape Colony, life at Prieska, a drought-stricken region bordering on the Kalahari, mostly Dutch and pitiably lonely, was very different from that at Keiskamma, nestling in the mountain land with its almost exclusively native population, or from life on the sheep farms of the gloriously open Karoo, the ostrich farms of the Klein Karoo or the fruit farms of the pretty south west. From Rhodesia southward, over the vast stretch of British Africa, little groups of two, three or more families banded together to support a teacher for their children and thus a farm school was established. It was precisely for such a school that Mother Cecile had started her training of teachers in Grahamstown.

The dilemma facing the Sisters and teachers at TC was how to prepare girls for such a situation while at the same time training them as competent and capable teachers. For this reason, there was the emphasis on a high sense of duty and a simple personal religion. The intention was to teach the students a little of many things thoroughly. They had to have a good knowledge of English, and Dutch if possible. They had to be able to teach the ordinary subjects, and drawing, needlework, music and singing. Then with that training and the prayers of the Sisters they went out to all parts of southern Africa to be teachers and much besides on the solitary farms of the land.

Dr EG Malherbe writing in his autobiography of his experiences from the 1920s admitted that of the students then being trained (in Cape Town where he was on the staff) hardly any were being prepared to function in a one- or two-teacher school in an isolated rural community and there were hundreds of such schools all over the country. Even those who had to train them lacked that first-hand experience.

The farm school was a single-teacher school of from five to twelve pupils. When the number exceeded twelve the school would be graded as a Third-Class School. The Education Gazette of 1905 explained that in a farm school the teacher did her work not on the lines of a class teacher but as a governess giving individual attention to her pupils. It was emphasised that the requirements of the standards were intended to be the same for all schools and that no extra leniency could be shown merely because a school was in a remote area and had few pupils. This was so that children moving from a farm school to a large school would not be at a disadvantage.

By 1905 there were 4172 children in farm schools in the Cape Province. The Department of Education was confident that with a qualified teacher it had been proved that excellent work could be done in a farm school. It was not unusual in a farm school to find pupils far older than might be expected for the particular standard and the Department felt that a good teacher would have the opportunity to enable the older child to recover lost ground.

The Cape Education Department laid down certain basic requirements for farm schools: there was to be a comfortable school room with a boarded floor and at least one window capable of being opened; there was to be a separate bedroom for the teacher, also with a boarded floor and a window; there were to be proper sanitary arrangements; and there was to be suitable furniture for the school room. It was pointed out to farmers that the comfort and well-being of the teacher would result in a well-run school.

The Department regularly received complaints about the accommodation provided for teachers and pupils. The Gazette for November 1911 carried a report of a court case where school was being conducted in a bedroom, the conditions being reported as totally unsuitable. Clearly the conditions in these farm schools varied greatly as did what was expected of the teachers. In some cases, the teacher was grossly overworked and what should have been a five-hour day ended up nearer to nine hours. This usually happened where there was more than one child who required private tuition in instrumental music. All this was then undertaken without any extra payment.

If the home was too far from the school, the children would be taken in as boarders by the farmer on whose farm the school was situated. This entailed the payment of boarding fees. These were worked out as follows: "For each boarder the farmer receives per month 1½ sheep, 1½ buckets corn, 1½ lbs coffee, sugar, rice, & soap. The child is expected to bring its own bed clothes. Often however 2 sheep per month are accepted in lieu of the contribution...and as a sheep in good condition is worth at present 23/- the year's boarding fee (holidays are excluded) may be placed at £24. The basis of calculation is simply what it takes to support the child, the extra trouble is not taken into account. Generally, there are three or four boarders, and the number of young people make it a lively house. The only person on whom the cares of life must fall somewhat heavily is the mother in charge."

In the first half at least of the twentieth century a considerable proportion of the elementary education of the land was entrusted to the farm school teacher. The farm school was no place for the specialist teacher. What was needed was someone who was bright and vigorous, who could do a little of many things thoroughly and adapt herself to widely different surroundings as the need arose. What the teacher would encounter on arrival at the farm was anyone's guess. One teacher was allotted part of an old church, in which the pulpit was still standing. Another used an old shed, a relic of the Anglo-Boer War, while another laboured in a disused barn. From the wilds of Rhodesia came news of life in a mud and pole hut lit by electricity and perilously near a crocodile-infested river.

There might be extreme loneliness, limited society and lack of entertainment. There was the strain of being at close quarters with pupils in school and home; there might be tears. On the other hand, youth is the time for courage and hope and though the prospect was somewhat daunting it brought with it a challenge.

An OG who had worked for four years as a farm school teacher and who returned to TC to further her qualifications wrote in the Magazine in 1913 of her experience. "I shall not mind at all if I have to go back to farm school work after my year here. On the whole, I shall prefer it. I like farms very well." She then adds, "There are doubtless a few difficulties in farm schools: e.gs: sometimes we have to teach boys older and taller than ourselves, and without knowing it, we may slip into a habit of conceit and arrogance; we get a bit out of fashion in clothes as well as in teaching... never fear, where the latter is concerned there is always TC to return to for a fresh store of knowledge."

As the years passed, fewer new teachers were prepared to teach in farm schools. In 1967 Sister Virginia wrote that every year she received desperate appeals from principals of small country schools begging her to get students interested in the post they had in many cases advertised without success. Students tended to apply for posts in the larger towns and few appeared willing to consider posts in small country towns and villages despite the fact that in those schools they frequently obtained excellent practice. They would find themselves having to cope with a small number of children possibly spread over a wide range of standards. This was not easy for any inexperienced teacher, yet students who tackled this job found it excellent experience and came to enjoy the life in a farming community. The last farm school under the control of the Education Department was closed on 30 June 1976. It was the Smoordrift farm school in the Bedford District.

TC-trained teachers and farm schools

The College Magazines give a fine picture of where the students ended up mainly in their first posting. The place of the Magazine in their lives was important and they happily wrote to tell how they were coping. The College Registers dating from 1894 record every student who entered the College, their age, home town, and course followed. They are a treasure trove, enabling one to compare where the students grew up and where they started work. These documents constitute a unique record of teaching in farm schools because of the strong links with the College and the way the OGs kept in touch. Here is a selection from the records to give an idea of what the students undertook:

Ella Impey (Born: 7-10-1883 at Salem. Student Number 138) taught at a school near Pretoria, "...a large government Farm School...all the children, except for four, are Dutch. They are very backward; they really know nothing at all."

Isabel Hoodless (Born: 11-3-1884. T3. No. 340) went from her home in Grahamstown to Matatiele: "I have 12 scholars at present, but Mr van Straaten thinks there will be more next quarter. It is quite enough though, for the beginning, as I have no proper materials or books and of those already ordered, nothing has as yet put in its appearance, but the bill. (Only managed to get some chalk today.)... The children's ages are from 4–12 years, five girls and seven boys, about five of them do not understand any English, and only two or three can talk it fairly well. However, I am getting along all right, and I like starting a school. I thought it would be dreadful. It is a pity, though, that the older ones have been out of school quite eight months, so you may imagine what a great deal they have forgotten." At a subsequent Inspection, the Inspector was most pleased with what he found, "The registers were well and neatly kept. The quality of the work was good and gave evidence of thorough and careful teaching, and although the inspection was held at an earlier date than last year, the results were excellent."

At Reddersburg in the Orange River Colony, Maria van den Hoven (Born: 6-7-1884 PT1. No. 210) whose home was in Rouxville, wrote that she had quite settled down in the new work and liked it very much. It was on a farm, two-and-a-half hours from Edenburg and one hour from Reddersburg. "I started school with eight pupils… I have to teach a big boy of 19 and a girl of 18…my pupils are all very backward, as they haven't been to school since the War, nor, indeed, during it, but they are such nice children and so anxious to learn, that it is a great pleasure to teach them. They are getting a new piano next week and I shall have five music pupils too." She also mentioned that in the evening, "I give lessons to a poor boy who is working here on the farm. I also have music pupils, a boy and a girl, much older than myself."

In the SGE Report for the year ending 1905 it was noted that, "In schools of the Farm School type, it is of great importance that the teacher should be musical and be able to teach singing. It means that a new element of enjoyment and self-culture is introduced into the monotonous life of the up-country farm. Only those who have spent a long winter evening in a remote Karroo farmhouse can realise what a difference music makes in the social life of the family."

One of the young women who had come out from England to train at TC ended up in the Willowmore district. She was Harriott Davies (Born: 1-11-1884. T3. No. 301. Home: England): "I am now on a farm, 24 miles from the nearest town, Post Office or station. I find it rather lovely out of school…there are only five children, but the eldest is in Std 6, the next in Std 5, the next in Std 3, and the two youngest in sub-standard. The school hours are from 9–12 and 2–4. After this I have music lessons to give, so my time is fully occupied…we have no near neighbours, so we have no change from day to day, save the weather."

Stofkraal A3 School near Marydale in the Prieska district was the place of employment of Edith Slater, whose home was in Sidbury. (Born: 29-10-1884. T2. No. 361.) It was a remote posting and involved a long journey from Prieska where she was met to the farm. "We left Prieska after breakfast, and I confess I found the journey very long and tiring… We spent the first evening at Marydale, our nearest PO... We travelled on the next day, only halting once we got to the Boegoeberg Waterworks. There we spent a few hours with the Second Engineer's wife. She is my nearest English neighbour (about 6 – 7 miles away) and has asked me to spend some weekends with her. We arrived at the farm at sunset."

She admitted that "it is some time since I spoke Dutch, and I found some difficulty just at first in conversation... I am sure you would be surprised if you could see my school room...an American organ, a glass case for museum, and a library consisting of 60 volumes...my predecessor was everything that a teacher should be. I have 17 children on the roll and my highest standard is the 6th. I have just finished making up my time-table, and I find it very difficult to keep all the children going. I can only do it by giving them rather long lessons." A later Magazine records that Edith had come prepared. She had brought some books from her father's library, so she had plenty to read, including Anson, *Voyage Round the World*, and *The Conquest of Granada*. She read to the children every afternoon, "...when I asked, 'do you understand what I read?' they would say most cheerfully, 'Oh no, but we like to hear you read'".

Edna Watermeyer, (Born: 20-4-1901. No. 1751. Home: Rouxville, ORC (Orange River Colony)) teaching at Rhodes in the Cape Province, "suggested to my class, that in order to improve their English, I should read stories to all those who wished to come on Friday afternoons. To my surprise, they all arrived, and seemed to enjoy the story, which we afterwards discussed."

Moving from Port Elizabeth to the Modder River (ORC) must have been quite an experience for Winifred Clarry (Born: 10-7-1883. KG. No. 89. Home: Port Elizabeth) but she was most positive about it. "I should like you to see the farm I am at now. It is a grand old place and it belongs to a Mr Fraser who is living here with his family. One of his daughters, Annie, left today for TC. I have been able to tell them quite a number of things they wanted to know about it, and I am never backward in talking of my old TC. I have come to the conclusion that I had better learn Dutch up here, for where I am at present, I have met only Dutch people, and one feels so strange to be in a room full of people and hear them talking and yet not understand what they are saying." She had trained as a Kindergarten teacher but was unable to use this as "the children are rather old; I am sorry for this, as I do love the KG work and methods... I hope we have some services on Easter Day; the Sundays without services are very lonely, but I am thinking of starting a little Sunday School next term."

Another brave lass was Amy Smith, (Born: 7-9-1886. T2. No. 385. Home: Alexandria), who went all the way from Alexandria to Steenbokfontein near Rustenburg in the Transvaal. "We started from Krugersdorp by post-cart at 5 a.m. on Sunday and arrived at Rustenburg at 3 p.m... The farmer had hired a cart and 4 mules from the PWD [Public Works Department]to convey me here, this place being 30 miles from Rustenburg. [Railway line not then in operation]. Our school room here is a good building...2 rooms... there is a cloakroom and a lavatory. The children I teach are in division 4 & 5 which corresponds roughly to our standards 3 & 4. Soon I shall have two Std 5 pupils and one Std 6. At present, some of the older pupils are at home, studying for confirmation, and will not be at school for another couple of weeks."

At the family where Amy Smith boarded nobody ever bathed. She used to be given a small basin of hot water every night to wash but she insisted on a weekly bath and as the family did not own a bath, every Saturday the children would be sent to a neighbour to borrow a zinc bath, which they would drag behind them over the veld. When Amy had had her bath, it would be returned over the veld behind the children.

The influence of the Dutch Reformed Church was clearly strong as was the draw of the bushveld for the farmers. "We are anticipating a very poor attendance this winter, as some of the farmers are leaving for the bushveld to shoot big game and are taking their families with them. One gets so disheartened over one's work sometimes because of the wretched attendance. One day the school rooms are full of children, and a day or two afterwards, there is only one third of the children present."

Amy said it was impossible to teach Physical Geography because the teacher was not believed. After she had taught that the world was round, a child came to the school next day and said: "*My Oupa sê dis pure bog* (nonsense). The Bible says that earth stands on pillars and you can't put a round thing on pillars!" Another disputed that the earth revolved because his grandfather had gone up in a balloon over Pretoria and when he came down he was still in Pretoria.

Martha Emslie (Born: 24-3-1886. T3. No. 278. Home: Seven Fountains) was at the Railway School at Thebus near Steynsburg. "I have nine boys and three girls in the school. The Inspector came today...all children passed... I cannot tell you how glad I am that my school has done so well, for I was wondering whether I had taught them all that was necessary for them to know, when lo and behold, I had taught them beyond what was required..."

At Renosterkop (nearest town Venterstad), Olive Wright (Born: 3-1-1887. T3. No. 410. Home: Queenstown) had 8 children, the two eldest in Std 2. She was learning the hard way! "I have made six time-tables and at last have one that seems to work well. During the week we speak English, and on Saturdays and Sundays we speak Dutch. We have school prayers and scripture every day, and I try to make it as interesting as possible... I think I am very fortunate; all are very kind to me...do all they can to make me happy."

Lemmie Hughes (Born: 8-10-1882. KG Elementary and Higher. No. 286. Home: Grahamstown.) found herself in the newspaper in Cathcart following an Inspection and the publication of the Inspector's Report. "The Kindergarten of this school takes its place amongst the best in the Eastern Province, but in no other school have such good results been obtained with so little assistance. The results could only have been achieved with the hard work and enthusiasm of the teacher in charge. We congratulate Miss Hughes, the KG mistress on the splendid report obtained by her at the last inspection...the KG department of any school is the most arduous department in the school, and the Cathcart School Committee should feel proud in having secured for this department the services of such a talented lady as Miss Hughes."

The language problem was encountered in a new way by Mabel Cockcroft (Born: 17-9-1888. PT1. No. 258. Home: Grahamstown.) She was teaching at Tzeli near King Williams Town and was helped by Miss Swain (the Inspectress) who "gave me some useful hints as to how to set to work among these little Germans. Most of the children are too big for much occupation work, so I have to make the Nature Study the main thing...I hardly realised at first that they were German and not English children; but I have begun to get used to their limited knowledge of English and can make them understand my meaning now."

Isobel Lennox (Born: 7-11-1898. T 3. No. 1782. Home: Fort Hare, Alice) found herself in a similar predicament at Keiskammahoek. "I have 33 children, mostly boys, and quite two-thirds of them are Germans. They are a very solemn little family and some of them seem only able to smile on very rare occasions. There are no pupil-teachers, so I have to manage the three classes alone the whole morning. I have two children who can speak only German and isiXhosa and do not know a word of English."

Nellie Key was endeavouring to teach in the vernacular at St Barnabas Mission at Mlengana in Pondoland West. (Ellen Georgina Key – Born: 30-6-1886. T2. No. 375. Home: Pretoria). "It is as much as I can do to struggle through a grammar lesson in isiXhosa. A click at the wrong end of the word makes such a difference... The mission is not well situated with regard to population."

One OG, Ethel Rait (Born: 1-5-1890. T3. No. 454. Home: Dordrecht) went all the way to Uganda to a school on the Uasia Gishu Plateau (via Eidome Ravine, East Africa Protectorate) "I am teaching again on a farm.

There are only five children at present and as they have been several years from school they are very backward...you would be surprised to see my school room. It is a papyrus house with a grass roof and the tables are made of forest wood. We are very near Mt Elgon...we are very far from anywhere."

Another, Joanna Loots (Born: 4-12-1898. No. 1811. Home: Middelburg), went to Okahanja in Ovamboland. She wrote that "at present I have 13 children from Sub A–Std 5 – all classes except Std 1."

Ann Wiggill (Born: 22-10-1900. No. 1754. Home: Sterkstroom) was appointed to Usakos, South West Africa. She described her new home as "a quiet little place. Most of the people seem to be employed in the railway workshops. The school is a wood-and-iron building, and not very convenient...Usakos is a 2-teacher school...living up here is very expensive, but we get a much better salary than we do in the Colony."

These young teachers were quick to remember the lessons drummed into them at College. Mabel Cotton (3-11-1880. 1 year at TC. No. 381. From Waterford, Ireland) at the Collegiate School for Girls in Port Elizabeth wrote: "I realise now, more than ever, how very helpful my year's training at the College has been to me...the practice of preparing notes, of lessons too, has made me quite quick with my preparation."

Another of the OGs even mentioned that after the Annual Inspection the Inspector had asked her if she had been at TC and "said he was glad the children were all successful, as the Sisters were always anxious to have the girls from the College doing thorough work."

Irene Buckley wrote to say, "When I received my first salary I remembered very well your advice to us before we left, so I was the proud possessor of 30 pounds for one hour only, after which I paid all my debts...and put what remained in the savings bank."

From the start of the Training School in 1894 the Sisters had stressed the importance of singing in schools. So it is interesting to notice that singing was an essential part of the curriculum in the schools where TC teachers were placed. Mattie Harney at Touws River even went so far as to organise a concert which had never been attempted before. "As soon as the inspection was over, I began teaching the children things for a concert. Most of them have never been to such a thing in their lives, much less acted in one, so it was a bit hard work, rubbing them into shape; but it was really marvellous how soon they got into the ways."

Frances Wormald (1-11-1887. KG. No. 391. Home: Tarkastad) teaching in Steynsburg sent a request "to Sister for suggestions re: a song book". It was just such a request that would lend itself to a useful article being printed in the College Magazine. Many of the OGs looked eagerly for their magazine to arrive. Sophie Reynolds writing from Burgersdorp mentioned: "I always look forward to the magazine...as it seems to bring with it a breath of the old College life." Joanna Louw, at Thomas River waxed lyrical: "Nobody can imagine how we all enjoy College news. I read the magazine through and back again; it was almost like having a letter from home."

The farm schools were as a rule in remote areas and the teachers needed some form of backup which they knew was always available to them at TC and through the Magazine. When Helen Schweppenhauser arrived in Bedford she wrote: "I found the magazine waiting for me, and I opened it almost at once and turned to the news of OGs; it was comforting to hear how the others were faring, and it made me feel much less nervous at having to meet so many new people." Writing from Molteno, Grace Cook recorded: "I received my magazine and did enjoy hearing all about college doings. It is such a link between past and present, and most inspiring as well as enjoyable to read of the doings of OGs as well as those at College." Grace Midgely (27-11-1900. T3. No. 2062. Home: Adelaide) writing from Alice was drawing up schemes of work for Nature Study and History and found the magazines most helpful in that regard.

A teacher in Barkly East, Iris Kriel, lent a colleague some past copies of the Magazine: "What a blessing the old mag is too! Always so helpful with its useful notes on teaching. A few months ago, I was glad to be able to help a teacher by lending her a few of my copies." Eveline Badger in Ugie, was at her wits end over her teaching of English – or failure to do so! "At first, I thought I should go mad – they were hopeless...but one day when I was reading all my old magazines, I came across a most useful article on 'How to teach English to Afrikaans children beginning English'. I devoured it and changed my scheme at once on the lines suggested. Really, the children have got on splendidly." Lizzie Truter took the advice incorporated in that article to heart and wrote that she had "followed the plan suggested of talking to the children out of school in the second language, and these conversations help them a great deal. It is surprising to see how quickly they pick up new words and phrases in this way."

Mary Long found a use for her First Aid knowledge when a little boy dislocated his elbow during playtime. He was wrestling another boy. Mary took him into the classroom, "pulled the arm so that the protruding bone jumped back into place with a click", then put the arm in a sling and sent the child home. This happened near Trumpeter's Drift.

May Van Zijl and Myrtle Carroll both concluded that real teaching is far divorced from the theory learnt in the text-book. May, based in Carnarvon, "arrived at the heart-breaking conclusion that during one's training one learns much which is theory alone and cannot be put into practice", least of all in small country schools. Myrtle had obviously had her unrealistic notions of teaching removed while teaching in Colesberg: she had had a great idea of ruling by love, but soon changed her tune.

One OG was to have a school named after her: Mary Waterton Waters – Born: 6-12-1886 at All Saints, Engcobo, Student No. 545, 1907–1908, Course KG Elementary. The School is in Grahamstown: the Mary Waters School.

Rhodesian [Zimbabwean] students

By the time of the Jubilee Celebrations in 1954 nearly 5000 students had been trained as teachers at TC. The influence they exercised on the minds of growing children is incalculable. The Second World War had brought an unexpected bonus to the College. Up to that point students desiring training as Primary School Teachers were sent from Southern Rhodesia to Britain to attend college. The escalation of the war, especially at sea, and the menace of the German U-boats, made it almost impossible to travel by sea. The Southern Rhodesian Education Department arranged with the Cape Education Department to send students to Cape training colleges. Twelve young women were allocated to TC. The Magazine for November 1940 recorded that they could be assured of a warm welcome. The Chief Education Officer for Southern Rhodesia, addressing the students at TC in 1944, mentioned that his Department had tried most of the training colleges in South Africa and some overseas but had concluded that the training at TC was the best they could get, and they wanted all their Primary teachers to train there.

The annual Rhodesian contingent at TC came to number in the region of 60 students and their presence made a huge impact on the College. The Rhodesian Government paid a *per caput* grant for their students. This was £12-10-0 per head per annum, undoubtedly a useful addition to the College income. Eventually the Rhodesian Government opened its own College in Bulawayo. The final batch of Rhodesian students trained at TC left in December 1960. Through the OGs contact was to remain as close as ever.

South West African [Namibian] students

Some students from South West Africa (SWA) attended TC from 1964 to 1975. A certain quota of SWA students had been allocated to each of the five Afrikaans-medium training colleges in the Cape and any English-speaking students would be sent either to the Cape Town Training College or to TC.

There is no record of OGs in Namibia holding reunions.

CHAPTER $\LARGE{11}$

Conclusion

O NE OF THE earliest works undertaken by the Community of the Resurrection of our Lord (CR) in 1893 after the Sisters opened the orphanage and started their own school was the training of young girls as pupil teachers. This led ultimately to the opening of the Training School and then the Training College. The closing of TC in 1975 marked the end of an epoch in the history of the Community. Up to this point the Community had been largely but not entirely a teaching order.

From 1975 the Sisters had no further contact with school teaching or the training of school teachers. This change came at a time when the Community was attracting few postulants or novices and even fewer teaching vocations. The nature of their work was to change entirely after their move from the St Peter's campus.

Clearly things had changed a great deal from the early days when the students were young girls of elementary school standard, fresh from the farms around Grahamstown. In 1975 students were far more sophisticated. Changes notwithstanding, TC had continued to produce fine teachers who were well trained and whose lives were enriched by the traditions of the

College. *Grocott's Mail* of 14 October 1975 drew attention to the fact that: "When Training College closes this term some 8,000 students will have passed through its halls and classrooms, with eight principals…to launch them on what has been a major contribution to South African education."

As an OG recalled: "We were so keen to go out and teach and we thought we knew enough to get by. Now thirty years later, I am still learning!"

Another OG wrote of her *alma mater*: "There is no doubt that there was something about our Training College that worked. There were lots of things that we rebelled against, but TC actually trained us well in our profession as well as maintaining certain standards and life skills."

Diane Emslie considered: "We were really privileged to attend TC where we were exposed to excellent tuition, and hands-on practical training. Youngsters today lose out not having those training colleges, as the universities simply don't offer the same training and the small-town colleges like TC and Graaff-Reinet had such a special aura."

For the students those last few years before closure were a mixed time as the numbers declined. Diane Emslie noted that as "we were the last TC students we grew very close, particularly in the 3rd year when it was only us left in two hostels (Cantab and Winch)! We did feel deprived in a way not having any 1st years to rag!" Miss Pilson the Principal (Rector) had a difficult time maintaining the *esprit de corps* of the remaining students.

"Our last few weeks were very sad and emotional, with final exams thrown in as well…When the doors were finally closed in December 1975, it was the end of an era and we were now part of history. We were privileged to learn at TC and the strong link between the Old Girls is evident." In those final years few leavers joined the OGG. "As College closed down, a lot of us did not join the OGG because we just thought it had all ended."

The outgoing students were given the opportunity to buy "furniture and crockery and other bits and pieces…We shed tears as we hugged and said farewells and looked forward to the next milestone in our lives that would be in a classroom putting into practice all we had learnt from that very special Training College."

In an editorial entitled "Changes", the editor of the College Magazine in December 1970 wrote that no one who had been through TC could leave without having assimilated the spirit and flavour of the place. There had been changes from the time it started. Change had become part of the fabric of the institution to keep pace with the changes in present day life and also with the changes and developments in education and training techniques.

In her speech at the final Founders' Day in October 1975 Mother Mary Eleanor CR gave thanks for the role which TC had played in the service of education in South Africa and beyond its borders. She spoke of the far-reaching influence of the College and of the OGs who had gone out to be educators carrying with them the indelible mark of the traditions and devotion which had made the College the unique institution it was. She spoke of the hundreds of students who had passed through the College and who had touched and influenced the lives of hundreds of children, who in their turn had influenced others, "and so it goes on – the building grows, and it is an enduring building because it is not made with bricks and mortar but of the characters and integrity of truly devoted women."

The College was a trail-blazer in many ways. It was indeed "an idea in the working". The idea was that of Dr Muir who expressed his hope on his first visit to Grahamstown that a teacher training institution would be opened in the city for the training of teachers for the Eastern Province of the Cape Colony. It was providential that in the audience that evening in the city hall was Mother Cecile of the Community of the Resurrection of Our Lord. She not only took note of that idea but turned it into a vision which she worked to fulfil.

Mother Cecile envisaged that the teachers trained at the School/College should then go out to the many farm schools of the interior taking with them not only their training as teachers but also their pattern of life as practising Christians. She was a broad-minded woman, and this was reflected in the atmosphere of the College. No one was debarred from entering the College on religious or denominational grounds. This was a remarkably enlightened view at a time when denominational differences were extremely evident. Roman Catholic and Jewish girls were likewise welcomed, and provision was made for their own religious observance.

Mother Cecile tried to play a part in bringing the two white communities together, by welcoming Dutch/Afrikaans girls to TC. This open-mindedness was to become a feature of TC and teachers leaving the College saw this as a legacy. OGs acknowledge that their three years at TC shaped their religious outlook and deeply affected their spiritual lives.

Mother Cecile wanted to train teachers who would be prepared to go out to the lonely parts of the Colony where good teaching at the time was lacking. They did this knowing they had something worthwhile to offer. The Sisters were never discouraged by the fact that after a few years the young women would find husbands and leave teaching. They felt that there was just as much teaching to be done within the family.

In conversation with OGs the writer learnt that many of them when their children were of school-going age were responsible for running the school for their local farming community in some cases for several decades. It was here that the early education was given before the children were sent off to boarding schools. The years spent in training were not lost to the profession in any way. It would be most valuable to have a definitive list of OGs who were responsible for running such Farm Schools. Such a list could then be added to the Official Archives at the Cory Library. Perhaps this could be a challenge for the various Guilds!

The role of Providence in the story of TC

It was *providential* that three people appeared on the stage at roughly the same time: Bishop Allan Webb, Cecile Isherwood, and Dr Thomas Muir. Allan Webb appealed for women to work in his Grahamstown diocese; Cecile Isherwood responded and agreed to come to Grahamstown in 1883 for three years. Dr Muir was SGE of the Cape Colony (a non-ministerial post) from 1892.

It was *providential* that sitting in the audience in the Grahamstown City Hall on the evening of 11 July 1894 was the same Cecile Isherwood by then Mother Cecile CR. The meeting was being addressed by Dr Muir, on his first visit outside Cape Town after his arrival in the country. Muir was a Scot – a Mathematician and a Classicist. He spoke of the need for a Training College in the eastern part of the Colony. Mother Cecile heard the appeal and responded. And so the Training School /TC came about.

Grahamstown Training College was the first in the Cape Colony to stress Class Music and Class Singing in schools, first to appoint a Physical Education teacher, first to employ a full-time librarian, first to employ an elocutionist. It was the only training college to have a Chapel. It was in the words of Sister Kate, a *unique educational development*: a privately-owned College, run entirely by an Anglican Religious Community, State Aided, Departmentally Inspected, and non-denominational in its enrolment.

It was *providential* that the Community of the Resurrection of our Lord grew in the numbers it did, and that out of those numbers there emerged a line of outstanding Sisters Principal: Clare, of whom it was said, Sister Clare is TC: she put the venture well and truly on its feet, and had Dr Muir round her little finger; Kate, who was a meticulous teacher and leader; Frances Mary, probably the greatest of them all; Truda, the one who began to feel the draughts where the College was concerned – under whose regime the first cracks began to appear; Virginia, who was to be the last of the line.

It was *providential* that the College even survived. It was never in a sound position financially. There was no capital; it was a hand-to-mouth existence for 81 years. Teaching Sisters' salaries were put into the building fund but when teaching salaries were increased they were used to bring lay teachers' salaries into line – the Department at first paid one third, then two thirds and finally full salaries. Before 1922 College and Community funds/accounts were operated as one; after that they were separated but the College was forever borrowing money from the Sisters, from the bank, from the Diocesan Trusts Board (DTB) – loans that had to be repaid. At times, even the smallest expenditure had to be debated. Students of course thought either the Community was extremely rich on TC money or that the CR should be more generous towards the College. When the money from the sale of the campus was received the first call was to pay outstanding loans.

It was *providential* that the College survived as long as it did. The number of teaching Sisters gradually diminished and finally dried up. Women were not offering themselves for the religious life in the numbers they once did. Two world wars had brought tremendous changes to society and to the place of women in that society. Women did join the Community; but those joining did not balance the number of those dying – and many who survived lived to a great age and were part of an increasing geriatric frail care. By 1969 there were no novices at all – the first time in the history of the Community.

It was *providential* that Rhodes University was undergoing an extraordinary expansion in the early 1970s and so the CR found a ready buyer for the College campus. Education policy stressed that training colleges should be attached to universities and comprise institutes of education numbering 800–1000 students. That was not a proposition for TC. By then there was only one teaching Sister on the staff and no Sisters in the hostels. The last Rectors were Mrs Enid Craig and Miss Bridget Pilson, an OG. They were loyal to the traditions of the College but there was no guarantee that the Department would continue to pay subsidies as in the past.

Grahamstown Training College was a unique institution in many ways not least in that it was run for most of the 81 years entirely by women, the eight principals being women of outstanding ability. At the time of writing it is over forty years since TC closed; those who attended in those final years are approaching retirement. The buildings remain as a special part of the Rhodes University campus but already the staff and students using them know nothing of their provenance. Mother Cecile's name is commemorated in the Mother Cecile Memorial Dining Hall, a fine structure by any standards and a worthy memorial to a remarkable woman whose influence on primary education in Southern Africa has been felt for more than a century.

Appendix

Years of service by lay staff

Miss Louw (Afrikaans) who retired in June 1964 after 21 years in the staff; Miss Bulbring, herself an OG, (Nature Study) on the staff for 30 years (1930–1960); Miss Temlett (Infant School Teaching) 1947–1960; Miss Stormont (English) 1950–1960; Miss Foster (Speech) 1950–1961; Miss Gillespie, another OG, (Music) who spent her entire professional life of forty-and-a-half years at TC, 1921–1962; Miss Winton (Physical Education) 1946–1964; Mrs Doreen Cillie, who retired in 1964 after 14 years; Miss Phyllis Dell (Domestic Science) 1956–1974; Miss Yvonne Eales (Needlework) January 1943–1973; Miss Lavinia Gentleman (Domestic Science) 1934–1950, 1954; Miss C Clarke: Matron Canterbury House retired in 1975 after 30 years' service; Miss C M Garnett: 1928, 1933–1952; Margaret Joyce McCrea (Music) 1938–1975 (38 years); Miss Stella Marneweck (Music) 1956, 1960–1975; Miss Patricia Marzo (Physical Education) 1960–1975. This constituted a remarkable record.

College Sisters

Sister **Dora** retired in 1930 after 30 years at the College. She was widely known as a successful trainer of Kindergarten and Infant School teachers. As a consequence, she had done "a lasting work for the country. Beginning with four students when the Department instituted the Course in 1903, she has trained a total of 684 teachers for Elementary or Higher Kindergarten Certificate, or (since 1917) for the Infant School Teachers' Certificate." "As in any specialised course success depends largely on the member of staff who is most identified with it, and responsible for giving it a unity, one must reckon this Sister Dora's solid contribution to the College work, and the teaching service in general." She was also active in social and sporting activities and college functions, and for a time filled the position of Vice-Principal. It was Sister Dora who attended the epoch-making Conference at Fort Hare in June–July 1930. This was the Bantu–European Students Conference, the first of its kind in South Africa. Among the speakers were Prof Edgar Brooks, Mr W G Bennie, Dr Jabavu, Dr MacMillan, and an Indian Professor from Ceylon, some of the foremost authorities on the subject of Race Relations. Sister Dora records that more than 200 students of all races were invited, among whom was a good contingent from both Stellenbosch and Fort Hare. It was the first time that such a considerable body of both Black and White students met together on equal terms. The intention of the Conference was to study the relations between "Bantu and European" (sic) in South Africa in the light of Christ's teaching.

Sister **Elsie** was on the staff for 20 years and was one of the long-serving members who had known Mother Cecile. Sister Elsie had been responsible in turn "for the 1st Year Class, a section of the 3rd Year, the T2 students and – for the last four years – the 1st Year T2s. Having fine intellectual powers herself, she has always expected a high standard of work from her classes and has been particularly successful in giving a thorough foundation to students in the 1st year – perhaps the most important year – of their training." She was an "intellectual giantess". She belonged to a group of Sisters who had at one time studied the Greek New Testament in their spare time, and "was never so happy as when she had a stiff theological book to read." While on the staff of the Training College, "she had a great influence, especially on the older students, and carried on her friendship with them long after they had left College." Like the Apostle St Paul, Sister Elsie had a thorn in the flesh: "at times one could see what an effort it was to carry on, as she suffered acutely from almost incapacitating headaches, the fruit of malaria in the tropical climate of her former labours...

Another Sister who had known Mother Cecile was Sister **Innes**. She was on the staff for 19 years. Sister **Bernadine**, who joined the staff as Miss Kibler, was another teacher who was well-known for the high quality of her work. She was attached to the Infant School Teachers' class, and there was a high demand for those she trained. Sister Bernadine was not bilingual, which created problems for the Education Department in that this was the only college training infant school teachers. The Principal had to write to the SGE, "(Sister Bernadine) is one of the most valuable teachers on the staff of this Training College...she has the personal qualities essential for the training of students. This teacher is a very competent trainer of infant school teachers, with excellent handwork and musical qualifications. She has made great efforts to acquire Afrikaans in holiday times and in any available spare time during the term; it is not easy...in an English environment. Great care has always been taken to safeguard the Afrikaans–medium work of the Infant School students, in literature and in teaching demonstration and practice." Sister Bernadine "was always so very human – so full of humour and understanding. I realise what grave responsibility rests upon all teachers...only our consistent and wholehearted following and continuing of her work can really honour her memory" was the comment of one who had been taught by her.

Sister **Margery**, who had been associated with Training College since 1917, retired in 1952. She was on the staff of the Music School. Sister **Mary**

Noel, before coming out to South Africa, had gone up to Somerville College, Oxford, with a Scholarship in Modern Languages. She was subsequently granted a Dublin M.A. on the strength of her Oxford studies. She then took a Cambridge Teacher's Diploma and Drawing Certificate. She arrived in Grahamstown in 1901, and immediately set about acquiring a higher Bilingual Certificate. She joined TC staff in 1912 and continued until 1919. She died in 1962, and her obituary notice recorded that "there are still OGs who remember her teaching with admiring gratitude".

Sister **Mary Christian** had fitted herself for a teaching career and arrived in Grahamstown in 1893 at the age of 24 and joined the staff of the Training School. She taught writing, drawing, and singing until the end of 1897. She re-joined the staff in 1904 and taught until 1908, acting for a brief period as Vice-Principal. "Her gift for writing delightful letters helped to gain many friends...she kept in touch with various old TC students." Sister **Eva** was a trained teacher, one of the first of Miss Beales' students at Cheltenham College; she joined the TC staff in 1902 and was remembered for her "sergeant-like" voice which rang across the grounds during PT lessons. It is interesting that as early as 1902 TC was already offering physical training. "(Sister Eva) was good at figures and was very good at helping those having less aptitude in that direction; and her advice was – always to teach for the dullest members of the class".

Sister **Katherine Maud** studied for (registered in 1906) and obtained the B.A. degree at Rhodes University College, and then taught at TC as the "member of staff chiefly concerned with the PT2 Classes in those days, though everyone met her in the Stationery room, and some yet again in the Orchestra." It is noted that one of her greatest gifts as a teacher was the understanding she had of the difficulties of the slower pupils, who by her bracing influence were often led to remarkable improvement. She was on the College staff from 1914 to 1947.

Sister **Elise** had taught in England before coming to Grahamstown in 1906. At TC, as a student, she took the PT2 course, coming second in the Colony. She was never to enjoy good health, but was able to teach various classes, including History of Education, though English was her first love. It was remembered that "her loving understanding of drama won splendid results". However, it was not in the classroom but in the Stationery Room and the Fiction Library that her real influence in the College was best felt. One OG wrote of her: "I was very often very sad to think she was suffering... She was always so very much alive, full of spirit and enthusiasm, and such a positive sort of person that it saddened me to see her so crippled and ailing... It was a great privilege to have known and loved her – I have very happy memories of her". Most of her life in the Community was spent at TC.

Sister **Lilian Frances** was the Art teacher. She was remembered as one who was always ready to welcome a new approach, something appreciated by her students. One OG, Bettie Moody (1940-1941) wrote of Sister's approach to art: "...although we loved and appreciated her at the time, it has been only over the years that one has come to realise how much she probably influenced our lives... instead of simply teaching us to draw and paint, she required that we put to paper our own impressions of what we saw and felt... because of her way of teaching I was able to get lovely free and uninhibited results from children". Sister Truda wrote of her high standards of work and of her being a most reliable member of the staff.

Sister **Dorothy Jane** had trained in England as a Physical Culture teacher; she arrived at TC in the early 1930s to be one of the early Gym teachers. Other Sisters with a long association with the teaching side of TC include: Sister **Dorothy** who retired in 1935 after 20 years at the College; Sister **Irene**, on the College staff 1913 to 1941, retired in 1941 after 29 years and Sister **Stella Mary**, 1914 to 1941. The College Magazine referred to Sister Dorothy's "untiring zest for new ventures in pedagogy". Among the Sisters who were involved on the Administrative side of the College, especially in the Bursar's Office, were Sisters **Beatrice**, **Paulina** and **Doris Mary**. The latter "was highly qualified for this post (of Bursar) and always enjoyed figures. She made a place for herself at College, not only with Bookkeeping (but) for her availability in any and every crisis. She could turn her hand to anything and was much loved by staff and students. When there was a change of Principal, Sister Doris Mary was the one who 'knew the ropes' and could be depended on to provide an answer in every situation."

Sister **Mary Eleanor**, who left the Bursar's Office to become the Assistant Superior, and then Superior and Mother of the Community, was in office when negotiations got under way for the purchase by Rhodes University of the Training College Campus. "Dr Hyslop soon realised that (in Mary Eleanor) he was dealing with a tough businesswoman. Beneath her saintly garb she was rigid in her demands for adequate compensation for the forfeit of an institution which had the highest reputation in South Africa in the training of primary school teachers." Such was the woman responsible for the College finances!

Sister **Charlotte Emily** never lost her delightful Irish wit which made her a real influence among the students. She was well-known for her "gracious dignity, which never failed her, even in the various calls and interruptions of the Bursar's Office, where she worked for many years."

Hostel Sisters

The Hostel Sisters who were able to exercise a notable influence on their young charges include the following: Sister **Valerie** in 1964 became House Sister of Canterbury House, and was seen by the students as "a woman of strong character (who) was well able to exercise discipline when necessary" (she was subsequently the Mother Superior from 1982 to 1991); Sister **Katherine Rhoda** helped in one or other of the College Hostels for some years; Sister **Muriel**, described by a student (unnamed) as "always gentle and so approachable"; Sister **Mary Joyce** was for a time House Sister of Canterbury, "many old students speak lovingly of her still..."(died 1930), the Dean of Grahamstown, at her funeral, spoke of her as possessing "the rare gift of making friends and winning hearts"; Sister **Beatrice** worked at Canterbury House under Sister **Joy** 1929–1930, and was House Mistress of Canterbury 1930–1933; Sister **Margery**, the much-loved teacher of class-music, was after her retirement House Sister of Bangor; Sister **Stella Mary** "quiet and unassuming, she was trusted and loved by numerous students... who kept in touch with her to her death in 1975".

Sister **Mary Christine**, House Sister of Lincoln, "received from her students the generosity which she herself poured out upon them; they all loved her and when the time came that she could no longer carry on, there was a real grief. OGs kept in touch with her for many years, and some right to the end of her life (1969)"; Sister **Martha** was the "much loved House Sister of Lincoln" and was another of the Sisters who kept in touch with some of the students she had there up to the time of her death; Sister **Ethelwyn** was influential as House Sister at Canterbury House. It was acknowledged that "the happiness and good discipline of this Hostel was, under her supervision, most marked, and the students were devoted to her". Before she came to South Africa, as a lay-person in England, she was a Probation Officer and head of a Rescue Home.

Sister **Amy** exercised her influence not in any Hostel but from the kitchen and the Cookery Lessons she gave to batches of students. "Sister Amy had a wonderful gift of getting hold of the older girls in the House, and not only of keeping in touch with them when they left, but of having a powerful influence for good over them. She understood them, and they learnt to trust her, and for many of them she was the main link with the Community in after years. They wrote to her of their lives and their doings, of their joys and their sorrows... As long as she was able to write letters, she would send sympathy and wise advice to all who needed it".

Sister **Ada Mary** in the early 1930s was the House Sister at Bangor and then at Canterbury from 1938–1945 and again 1952. Her students recognised her "large-heartedness and sense of joy and fun (which) stand out as her predominant qualities. How she mothered the students in her care! How she entered into all their joys, their troubles, their home interests, and their family life! She was elderly in years but young in spirit"; Sister **Lilian Frances** (Sister Lil to the students) was House Sister, first of Truro and then Winchester. An OG, Beth Denton (1944–1946) wrote of her: "She was more than a mother to me, she was a true and loving friend, and hours in Truro were far more flexible than they had ever been in Lincoln... In the House there was always time for talk... When I left College in 1946, parting from her was like leaving one of my own family. We continued to write to each other and her letters were a delight." Another OG, Margie Antrobus (Gordon, 1966–1968) wrote: "We all had great respect for Sister Lil... the listener and spiritual carer of the girls of Winchester." Another OG, Janet Rice (Scorer), remembers Sister Lil as "wise beyond words, and oh, so forgiving." She writes, "We were always thrilled to arrive back at Winchester and into the arms of our wonderful Housemistress, Sister Lil. There was always tea or coffee, and those legendary TC biscuits..." Sister Lil retired in 1970.

Sister **Benedicta**, House Sister of Bangor, "where she was loved and much respected, although she was a firm disciplinarian"; Sister **Winifred Mary** was House Sister of Lincoln Hostel for over four years. It is recorded that she had a happy relationship with the students there, and right up to the time of her death (in 1989) they were writing to her and visiting her, for they appreciated her caring concern for them; Sister **Dorothy Jane** was in charge of Bangor in the late 1960s, where she was much appreciated. "She really understood young people, listened to them, and entered into their difficulties, their joys and their sorrows. Boy friends were equally at their ease with her"; Sister **Leila Mary** whose obituary notice reads: "Although brought up in a strict Victorian home, she was wonderfully understanding of modern youth and its difficulties, and was much beloved and trusted as a College House Sister, where she continued to work as a House Sister up to the age of 80... College missed her, but many students kept in touch with her until the end..."

Lists of House Sisters

In each Hostel of approximately 50–60 students, there was a House Sister in charge. The Matron helped the House Sister with Hostel duties for students and was responsible for the three servants who looked after the students' rooms, and was also responsible for the bed linen, etc. in her house.

Canterbury House

1936–1937: Sister Christine
1938:   Sister Doris Mary
1939–1945: Sister Ada Mary
1946–1949: Sister Ethelwyn (Novice)
1950:   Sister Hildegarde (Novice)
1951–1954: Sister Ethelwyn
1955–1957: Sister Joyce Mary
1958–1960: Sister Veronica Joy (Novice)
1961:   Sister Patricia
1962:   Sister Beatrice May
1963–1966: Sister Valerie Mary (Novice)
1967:   Ms Marjorie Wright – Lady Warden
1968:   Sister Mary Barbara
1969–1974: Ms Marjorie Wright – Lady Warden
1975:   Miss Mary Hall – Lady Warden

The Grotto

1916–1917: Sister Rhoda (1917 with Sister Martha & Sister Laeta)
1918–1921: Sister Innes (1918 with Sister Laeta & Sister Rose)
1922:   Sister Elise
1923:   Sister Stella Mary (with Sister Hilary)
1924:   Sister Rose
1925–1928: Sister Stella Mary
???
1932   Sister Perpetua

Bangor House

(Entry in Log Book, 29 January 1923: Bangor House not quite ready owing to strike difficulties. Girls distributed round other Houses for the first two or three days.)
1923–1926: Sister Dora (1925 with Sister Benedicta; 1927 with Sister Mary Bernard)
(Log Book for years 1932–1942 Lost)
1939–1941: Sister Stella Mary
1942–1947: Sister Doris Mary (1947 with Sister Margery)
1948:   Sister Mary Elizabeth (Novice)
1949:   Sister Mary Eleanor (Novice)
1950–1951: Sister Jennifer (Novice)
1952–1961: Sister Leila Mary (1961 with Sister Bertha)
1962:   Sister Moira Dorothea

1963:   Sister Jennifer
1964:   Sister Barbara (to June) Sister Margery (from July)
1965–1969: Sister Dorothy Jane (September–December 1966 Sister Erica Elizabeth)
1970–1972: Sister Mary Anthony (1971 January to June, Sister Dorothy Jane)
1973–1975: Miss Swart – Lady Warden

Winchester House

1951–1954: Sister Hildegard Mary (with Sister Helene Mary)
1955:   Sister Esther Madeline
1956–1959: Sister Barbara
1960–1969: Sister Lilian Frances
1970:   Sister Pamela Mary
1971–1972: Sister Lilian Frances
1973–1975: Miss Wiseman – Lady Warden

Lincoln House

1960–1962: Sister Winifred Mary
1963–1964: Sister Christine
1965–1967: Sister Pamela Mary (Novice)
1968–1970: Sister Margery